Paula White has shared words with our church that changed us forever. Whoever gets a chance to experience her fresh approach to ministry coupled with her deep love for broken people will never be the same again. Paula White will leave an indelible imprint on her generation with this book.

—T. D. JAKES
THE POTTER'S HOUSE
DALLAS, TEXAS

HE LOVES ME

He Loves Me Not

PAULA WHITE

WHAT EVERY WOMAN

NEEDS TO KNOW ABOUT

UNCONDITIONAL LOVE

BUT IS AFRAID TO FEEL

HE LOVES ME

He Loves Me Not

Charisma®
HOUSE
A STRANG COMPANY

Most STRANG COMMUNICATIONS/CHARISMA HOUSE/SILOAM products are available at special quantity discounts for bulk purchase for sales promotions, premiums, fund-raising, and educational needs. For details, write Strang Communications/ Charisma House/Siloam, 600 Rinehart Road, Lake Mary, Florida 32746, or telephone (407) 333-0600.

HE LOVES ME, HE LOVES ME NOT by Paula White
Published by Charisma House
A part of Strang Communications Company
600 Rinehart Road
Lake Mary, FL 32746
www.charismahouse.com

Unless otherwise noted, all Scripture quotations are from the King James Version of the Bible.

Scripture quotations marked AMP are from the Amplified Bible. Old Testament copyright © 1965, 1987 by the Zondervan Corporation. The Amplified New Testament copyright © 1954, 1958, 1987 by the Lockman Foundation. Used by permission.

Library of Congress Cataloging-in-Publication Data
White, Paula M. (Paula Michelle)
     He loves me, he loves me not / Paula White.
     p. cm.
ISBN 0-88419-565-1 (alk. paper)
1. Christian women—Religious life. 2. Love—Religious aspects-Christianity.
3. White, Paula M. (Paula Michelle) I. Title.
BV4527.W478 1998   98-39130
248.8'43—DC21   CIP

04 05 06 07 08— 10 9 8 7 6 5 4 3 2 1
Printed in the United States of America

Dedication

This book is dedicated to my wonderful husband, Randy. It is because of you that this message will bring freedom and love to so many others. You have been the instrument that God chose to use to bring healing and restoration to my life. Thank you for always believing in me and seeing the best in me, even when I could not. You are my best friend, my mentor, my companion, my ministry partner, my lover, my pastor, and the most incredible man in the world to me. I love you and respect you more than words could ever tell!

Acknowledgments

First and foremost, thank You, Lord, for rescuing me and making my life fulfilling. Every day is exciting because of You. I love You forever.

To my husband, Randy, who discerned the call of God on my life and continually "stirs up the gift of God" within me. Thank you for your patience, understanding, and encouragement for me to complete every assignment on my life.

To my precious son, Brad, who brings great joy to my heart. I am so proud of you.

To the staff at Without Walls International Church and Paula White Ministries. You are the greatest! Thank you from the bottom of my heart for your faithful diligence in bringing the vision to pass. I pray the abundance of God's blessings to overtake you.

To the Charisma House staff, who have labored alongside of me to complete this project. You are a tremendous blessing. We love and appreciate you, Joy and Stephen Strang.

To Lela Gilbert, who has inspired me and helped pull my thoughts together. Thank you for contributing your gift to this message.

To my extended family and friends, whom I love and appreciate.

To all the adversity I have had to face. I would never know that God would solve my problems if I had never faced any.

Contents

ONE

The Heart of a Woman

A pretty African American lady hastily came into my office for a 3:00 P.M. appointment that she had scheduled with me that very morning. I had no idea why the urgency for meeting. She sank into the chair, looking nervous and distracted. As we joined hands in prayer, I asked God to direct me, guide me, and give me wisdom to speak forth the mind of Christ during our meeting.

"What can I do for you?" I calmly asked her after our brief time of prayer.

"Why don't they love me?" she blurted out.

My puzzled facial expression must have indicated to her my need for further explanation. As the tears began to well up in her eyes, she repeated, "Why don't they love me?"

"Who?" I gently asked.

"Everybody!" was her heartfelt answer.

As I probed further, her story came out in bits and pieces. Her root of rejection began as a child when her mother had given her away to someone else to raise her, but had kept her brother. Sobbing uncontrollably, the distraught woman interrupted herself to again ask me, "Why didn't they love me?"

"Tell me more..." I encouraged.

She began revealing to me a series of events that took place in her life after her mother had abandoned her. She had begun a quest, as saying goes, "looking for love in all the wrong places." A boyfriend, a foster parent, a lover, a husband, anyone—she just wanted to be loved. She had jumped from relationship to relationship crying out, "Somebody, please love me!"

As far as she was concerned, no one had ever answered.

"Why Didn't Daddy Love Me?"

One Sunday evening at our church altar, I came alongside a lovely woman. Her outside, "Barbie-like" appearance gave her the persona of being a well-rounded person, but when I touched her shoulder to minister to her, she nearly collapsed in my arms. She put her head on my shoulder and began to sob deeply.

Somebody, please love me!

In between deep gasps for air she all but screamed, "Why didn't he love me?"

Her pain was so intense I could feel it deeply myself.

"Who didn't love you? Who was he?" I asked the questions quietly, almost afraid to hear her answer.

"Why didn't my daddy love me?"

The woman told me a tragic story of a cold and detached father's repeated rejections. After years of cruelty, he walked out of her life, never to return again. And although she was nearly forty years old, I felt as if I were holding a five-year-old girl in my arms. She could not stop crying as she repeated again and again, "All I wanted was for him to love me."

An Unloving Husband

My lunch conversation with a well-educated and attractive middle-aged woman turned very serious long before we had finished eating. She told me how she often stood before her bedroom mirror staring at her reflection and crying uncontrollably, asking, "What is it about me that is so unlovable?"

This woman had been widowed, and now she was remarried for the third time. "This man," she explained with a tearful smile, "is my one true love. I've never felt this way about anyone else. I thought we would live happily together forever, but then something went drastically wrong."

After seventeen years of marriage, her "one true love" had announced, "I don't love you anymore!"

Now, as she explained her predicament to me, my friend could not stop the tears that flooded her cheeks. She told me that she had been crying for weeks, maybe even for months now. And day after day as she stood gazing into that mirror, she noticed the lines on her forehead, the wrinkles around her eyes, and the gray hair that had replaced the brown. She was frightened, realizing that her life had gone by like a vapor. As she cried, she confessed, "All I ever wanted was someone to love me. And I don't think anyone ever has."

The Cry of Every Woman

It is an all too familiar cry. It was my own cry for years, and I believe it is the heart cry of every woman: "Somebody, please love me!" Most women desire love more than anything else. A woman's longing to be loved is natural: It is a God-given desire to want love and to want to give love. Problems and conflicts may arise, emotional highs may sweep us off our feet, but we never stop pulling the petals off the daisy, whispering quietly, "He loves me, he loves me not…" as we pray that things will turn out all right.

Why are we so desirous of love? Are we just needy, helpless creatures who can't live without a man to take care of us? Not at all! According to God's Word, there is a far more significant reason for our emotional makeup: God made women to give and receive love. When God made man (Adam), He said, "It is not good that the man should be alone; I will make him an help meet for him" (Gen. 2:18).

Our Creator recognized the need for Adam to have a counterpart, a companion, someone to share love with him. This is interesting, because it was God who placed Adam in the garden, in the middle of paradise, and Adam was not complaining about being lonely. He was not grumbling or griping about needing anything or anyone. Adam was a "happy camper."

It was God who decided that Adam was going to need a helpmeet. Why? Because God knows His human creature. He had created Adam in His image. Although Adam could not recognize his needs at this point, God knew that Adam had been created with a desire for love.

Maybe you think that you don't want love or even need love. Maybe you have the idea that you're the exception—God didn't create *you* with a desire to be loved. Maybe you don't want an encore of the pain, hurt, or rejection you've experienced before. Maybe you don't want to repeat some bad situation you encountered while looking for love, but *you do want love.*

Desiring love is our most basic instinct.

It is imperative that you understand you have an enemy in your life. His name is Satan.

> Be sober, be vigilant; because your adversary the devil, as a roaring lion, walketh about, seeking whom he may devour.
>
> —1 PETER 5:8

The Bible tells us not to be ignorant or unlearned of Satan's wiles: "Lest Satan should get an advantage of us: for we are not ignorant of his devices [wiles]" (2 Cor. 2:11). *Wiles* means "plots, plans, and schemes." Satan has come to kill, steal, and destroy you. Jesus explained, "The thief cometh not, but for to steal, and to kill, and to destroy: I am come that they might have life, and that they might have it more abundantly" (John 10:10).

Because of your unique design as a woman, part of Satan's plan of destruction for your life is that you never develop "healthy" relationships. He will send demonic assignments in your life when you are five years old to keep you messed up when you are fifty years old. He is the one who instigates the destruction in your life. He is the one who sends the pain to rob you of your emotional strength. Recognize that it is your enemy—and God's—who has tried to damage all of your relationships.

Ephesians 6:12 states, "For we wrestle not against flesh and blood, but against principalities, against powers, against the rulers of the darkness of this world, against spiritual wickedness in high places." Satan has a purpose for wanting to distort and damage your view of a healthy and whole relationship.

I once read of a study that was performed on sick babies. From the time of birth until they reached approximately one year of age, half of the babies were placed in incubators throughout their recovery. These babies were pretty much removed from the human touch. The other half of the babies were nurtured and held by caregivers twenty-four hours a day. The infants that were held, talked to, and cuddled not only recovered faster from their illnesses, but they developed much more quickly both physically and emotionally.

Satan knows that you need to be loved, held, and cared for. And if he had his way, he would disrupt the process of those needs being met by destroying every relationship in your life.

Men at Work, Women in Love

Relationships are vital to the development of the whole person. If my natural father abandons me, I will probably have difficulty receiving my heavenly Father's love. If my husband mistreats me, then I will probably have difficulty understanding and receiving the love of God. Because of my negative earthly relationships, I will have a tainted image of God and who He is. I believe that one of the reasons God told the man to love his wife as Christ loves the church was to strengthen and support a woman's concept of God. (See Ephesians 5:25.)

Many women have a tarnished view of love because the male figures in their lives have mistreated them. Therefore, these women have a problem accepting and believing in God's love. Women often cannot "feel" God's love because of these damaged relationships. Thus, their relationships with both God and with others are deficient.

For the most part, damaged relationships affect women to a greater extent than men. Now don't get me wrong—men need love, nurturing, and warmth, too. However, they have different requirements and responses to love than women. Let me show you in the Word of God what I mean.

When God created man, the first thing He gave him was a job (Gen. 2:15). Before Adam had a wife or family, he had responsibilities. He woke up to work. Adam was birthed into position and productivity.

When God created Eve, she was created as a helpmeet to Adam. She woke up as a wife. She was birthed into relationship. Can you imagine waking up "a wife"? She woke up to "Honey, where are my socks?" and to "Get me the grits." No wonder Eve took a walk in the garden and lent her ear to Satan. The girl was probably all stressed out!

*W*omen are fulfilled through relationships while men are fulfilled through achievement, career, or position.

When Adam and Eve disobeyed God's instruction, that disobedience brought forth sin, which brought forth death. Their disobedience caused humanity to fall and brought a curse upon us all. When the Fall occurred, it compounded the existing situation. In Genesis 3:16, God said unto the woman: "Thy desire shall be to thy husband, and he shall rule over thee." In other words, the woman would be relationship oriented. In Genesis 3:17–19, God told Adam that the ground, which was his job, would be cursed and "in the sweat of thy face shalt thou eat bread." That's another way of saying that man would be work oriented.

That is why women are fulfilled through relationships while men are fulfilled through achievement, career, or position. If I want to destroy a woman, I will attack and damage her relationships.

If I want to destroy a man, I will attack and damage what he does.

Have you ever noticed that if you ask a woman who she is, her response will be that she is the mother of this child or the wife of that man? She will tell you all about her relationships. If you ask a man who he is, he will tell you what he does.

When a woman is with her friends and needs to go to the bathroom, she thinks nothing of announcing it and inviting a friend to join her. Most women are perfectly happy to flock together to the bathroom. A man, on the other hand, would rather burst before he goes to the bathroom with another man!

It is said that a woman needs a minimum of thirteen touches a day just to survive emotionally. A woman will speak an average of twenty-five to fifty thousand words per day in comparison to a man's mere fifteen to twenty-five thousand words. Women need someone to touch them and to talk to them to develop a healthy self-esteem. Women are relationship oriented.

On the other hand, if you take away a man's job and his ability to provide for his family, you interfere with his self-esteem. Man had position with God before he had relationship with any other human being. Consequently, men are much more concerned about position, power, titles, and status than women normally are. A large part of a man's self-gratification comes from what he does.

Because of our fundamental differences, our expressions also vary. Women tend to be emotionally stimulated, while men are sight stimulated. Men are hunters. They see and conquer. Women, being emotional, need to feel. That is why when we come together intimately a man is stimulated by what he sees while a woman is stimulated by how she feels. That's the way God created us.

I have seen many women struggle to compete for attention with their husband's job. This is so damaging to a relationship, and it is not necessary. Your man needs his career position just as much as you need him.

When I first discovered this marked difference between men and women illustrated in the Word of God, and I understood that this is how God created us, I had mixed emotions. I was glad finally to understand why we are so different in many ways, but I was frustrated that my mate would not share my relationship-oriented desires. Then I figured it out. If we were both relationship oriented, we would never get anything accomplished. So, while he is chasing his position, I am chasing him!

We pick on Eve a lot. Many of us have stated self-righteously that *we* never would have eaten from the tree of the knowledge of good and evil in disobedience to God. I have compassion for Eve. She has taken the heat from a lot of people. I feel for Eve because although she had been created in perfection, with all the knowledge and skills necessary to fulfill her role as Adam's helpmeet, she had never had to put those skills to use in the face of the opposition and temptation from the enemy.

Since the Fall, we are no longer created in perfection as Eve was. We no longer have the know-how to fulfill our roles perfectly. For women, the instinct and desire to give and receive love is there, but the know-how must be developed. Many times this takes place based on what we have seen or experienced, which is often dysfunctional. As a result, we pattern and carry out behavior that will produce damage to our relationships; the offspring or recipients of those relationships will then have a distorted and damaged view of a "healthy" relationship. This is so important to understand, because how I relate to those around me affects how I relate to God. How I relate to God affects how I relate to myself, which affects how I relate to those around me.

Learning From Leah

So how do we break this vicious cycle that creates unhealthy relationships? First of all, we must get God involved. We cannot know and love others until we know and love ourselves. And we cannot fully know who we are until we know who God is. My understanding of myself and my understanding of God are closely intertwined.

Many people base self-perception on someone else's point of view or perception of them. In other words, if someone's perception of them is negative, their self-image is wounded. As God's adopted children, we need to see ourselves from His perspective: *I am not who others say I am; I am who God says I am.* But sometimes that is easier said than done.

What if, for example, you are in a situation where you cannot make another person love you, appreciate you, or value you? In Genesis 29:15–35 we find the story of a woman named Leah who was faced with that very problem.

Jacob, Isaac's son, had been running for his life. He had gone to live at his Uncle Laban's house. Laban was Leah's father. The Bible records that when Jacob got there, he saw Rachel and fell head over heels in love with her. Rachel was beautiful in form, countenance, features, and appearance. Whatever bug bit Jacob got him real good, for he agreed to work for Laban for seven years if he could marry Rachel.

At the end of seven years, Jacob entered the bedchambers on his wedding night, only to be deceived by Laban. Now remember, Jacob himself is a trickster, a con man. His very name, *Jacob*, means "deception." But here was someone who could outfox him. As the Word says, "Be not deceived; God is not mocked: for whatsoever a man soweth, that shall he also reap" (Gal. 6:7). The

Bible says that Leah was timid, weak, and cross-eyed. It was the custom for the bride to be veiled and the bedchamber dark. The bride did not take off her veil until the next day. When Jacob saw Leah's face the next morning, he was horrified—Laban had tricked Jacob and given him Leah, Rachel's sister.

I can imagine that Jacob whispered sweet nothings in his bride's ear all night long. He must have made love to her with a passion—any man who is going to wait seven years is going to be passionate. He thought he was kissing the woman who was the love of his life, only to discover the next morning, when she lifted the veil, that it was Leah—old cock-eyed Leah.

Jacob ran back to Laban, wildly complaining that he had been deceived. After some negotiation, he entered into an agreement to work another seven years for Rachel. In the meantime, Leah attempted to win the love and affection of her husband.

Can you imagine? Leah was caught between the manipulation and deception of two master tricksters. Meanwhile, all she wanted was to be loved. Was that too much to ask? That is all women really want—someone to love, admire, and respect us. Jacob had been passionate with her all night long, but when she awoke the next morning, longing to be held by her husband, she faced an empty bed. She was left alone and rejected. Feelings of being used, abandoned, unwanted, and undesired must have overwhelmed her. Can you imagine how it feels to be someone's booby prize? From the pit of rejection, Leah began her quest to win Jacob's heart. In her desire to win her husband's affection, the Bible says that she decided to have children.

Leah gave birth to her first son and named him Reuben. *Reuben* means "to look, to see." When she named him Reuben, Leah was saying, "Pay me some attention." There are many things we do to get attention. Anyone who lives in an environment where adequate attention is not given will use "attention-getters." This is normal—we all desire attention.

Leah's attention-getter tells me that Jacob did not notice if Leah had on a new or an old dress or if she had gained or lost weight. Many marriages suffer today due to a lack of attention. Women cry out silently, "At least show me that you know I am in this house." "Let me know that I am more important than that ball game or that computer!" "Somebody, please notice me!" So Leah named her firstborn *Reuben*—"LOOK!...Look what the Lord has given me!" She thought that having a boy and naming him Reuben might cause Jacob to look at her.

> *We* cannot fully know who we are until we know who God is.

Can you imagine the frustration of always trying to get the attention of someone who constantly ignores you and acts as if you don't exist? It does something to your spirit; it crushes you and messes with your psyche. Eventually you conclude that there's something wrong with you; that is why you are being ignored.

When Leah still failed to get the attention of her husband, she decided to name her second child Simeon. *Simeon* means "to hear." She thought, *If he won't look at me, then maybe he will listen to me.* It is terrible to be ignored. It does something to your personality. Many of us have experienced the type of situation where we are constantly begging people to listen to us. "I have something to say!" "I'm important; don't ignore me while I talk!" "Listen to me!"

But Jacob did not listen to Leah, so she named her third son Levi. *Levi* means "to be joined to, to be connected with." She thought that naming her son Levi might persuade her husband to hook up with her, to become intimate, that they could become as one. After all, isn't that what marriage is all about? Obviously a separation existed between Jacob and Leah—there was never really a joining together.

You can have a ring and a piece of paper and never really have a marriage, because a piece of jewelry and a license do not constitute intimacy and commitment. You can sleep in the same room and in the same bed and not be one flesh! And every now and then you want to have a "Levi"—you want to be connected.

This poor woman simply could not get what she wanted and needed from a husband who did not love her. How do you handle situations that are so adverse? What do you do when you cannot control a person's emotions and attitude? When you cannot make a person love you, respect you, or even speak to you, what do you do? *You get God involved!*

Leah finally wised up. When she could not get Jacob's attention or get him to listen or be intimate with her, she named her fourth son Judah. *Judah* means "let Jehovah be praised!"

When you are tired of people ignoring you, not wanting to be around you, and really not caring about you, then it's time to switch gears. It is time to have yourself a "Judah." Let Jehovah be praised! That is when you decide, "I don't need your attention to survive. You don't have to listen to me or be hooked up with me. I am going to birth myself a Judah; I am going to praise God!"

Another Woman in Search of Love

God is worthy of your praise. He sees you; He listens to you; He knows you intimately; and He wants to make you whole. He created you as a woman who thrives on relationships, and He wants every relationship in your life to be complete. But it must start with Him. Do you remember the woman at the well of Samaria in John 4? She had been in five marriages and was now living with a man. One of the signs of dissatisfaction with one's self, or of a low self-esteem, is going from relationship to relationship. This woman was empty. Maybe you are empty, too.

When Jesus approached her He told her to "drink" of Him first, and He would satisfy her longing. He was telling her that He could do for her what five husbands had not been able to do—satisfy her! If you will put God first and go to Him for what you want most, then and only then will you experience wholeness. I know that what I'm saying is true, because I have firsthand experience.

I know what it is like to feel abandoned, cast aside, and unloved. I know how important love is to a woman. Most of all, I have experienced some amazing and wonderful things about God's love. Yes, God *can* answer the cry of a woman's heart. He answered Leah's. He has answered mine, and He will answer yours. In the pages that follow, I hope you will find out exactly what His love can do. I've discovered that when a woman says, "Won't somebody please love me?" God is waiting to answer: "I will love you. I do love you. I have loved you all your life, and I always will."

Personal Reflections

Think About This

Read the quotes from this chapter below. After each one take a moment to reflect on how the statement links to a feeling or experience in your own life. Give your own personal reaction to each statement.

1. Most women desire love more than anything else. A woman's longing to be loved is natural: It is a God-given desire to want love and to want to give love. How has this desire been evident in your own experience?

2. Because of your unique design as a woman, part of Satan's plan of destruction for your life is that you never develop "healthy" relationships. He is the one who sends the pain to rob you of your emotional strength. Recognize that it is your enemy—and God's—who has tried to damage all of your relationships. Describe how his destructive plan has impacted your life.

3. God is worthy of your praise. He sees you; He listens to you; He knows you intimately; and He wants to make you whole. He created you as a woman who thrives on relationships, and He wants every relationship in your life to be complete. But it must start with Him. List the ways you are trying to center primary relationships in your life on God and His will for you.

Talk to God

Lord, thank You for making me the woman that You have called me to be. Thank You for understanding me when I have felt misunderstood and unloved by others. Thank You for loving me. At times, I have run to the wrong arms, looking for love in the wrong places, but You have never given up on me. You have always met me when I have turned back toward You, and You have drawn me closer than ever to Your heart. Thank You for always seeing me, always hearing me, and always desiring to have an intimate relationship with me. I praise You for enabling me to see myself as You see me—as a woman designed by You to give and receive love and as Your beloved child. Amen.

TWO

"Paula, You Are Unlovable!"

My mother, my brother, Mark, and I hadn't lived in Memphis long when, one terrible night, I heard a knock on the front door. At first I was excited to hear my father's familiar voice, but it did not take long for me to realize that it sounded hard and cold. Gone was the warm sweetness I had always loved.

A few words of conversation were exchanged. Then suddenly, in a panic-stricken tone, my mom screamed, "No! You can't have her! Absolutely not!"

The next thing I knew, one of my arms was being yanked and pulled by Daddy, and the other arm was being pulled by Mommy. My parents were fighting over me like a rag doll in a tug of war.

"Give her to me!" Daddy shouted desperately.

"No! I will never give her to you," Mom vowed with terror in her eyes. Her grip tightened.

One of Daddy's hands was holding me tightly. With his

other hand—the hand that had protected me, poured syrupy smiley faces on my pancakes, and held my feverish hand in a hospital emergency room—he began to knock my mother's head against the wall with brutal force.

Mom screamed to my brother, "Call the police!"

They continued fighting and exchanging ugly words. I heard Daddy say, "Let me have her, or I'll kill myself! If I can't have you or her, I don't want to live!"

"No!" she screamed. With every ounce of her strength she held me as if she were holding on to her own life. Then it was over. The police came and took him. "We'll lock him up until he sobers up," the officer informed my mom. I had no idea what "sober" meant. But somehow I knew I would never see my daddy again. I was five years old.

It wasn't long before the phone call came. I answered it and heard a man's voice on the line. I didn't recognize it; it was cold and distant, inquiring, "Is your mother available?"

"Mommy, it's for you!" I handed her the phone and watched her face with growing curiosity. She grew pale. She put her hand over her mouth and braced herself. When she hung up the phone, tears began to pour down her cheeks, and she grabbed me and held me so tight that I thought she would suffocate me. It seemed as if she would never stop crying.

"Your daddy's dead," she finally told me.

It was true. My father had killed himself just as he had vowed to do if he couldn't have me. He had driven his car into a tree and had been pronounced dead on arrival at the hospital.

Daddy's Little Girl

Until that night, until that horrible phone call, I had lived a charmed life. As far as I could see from my child's perspective, I was the most fortunate little girl in the world. I still recall the daily rituals that always began with breakfast in a nice restaurant. Daddy was smiling, "What do you want to order today, Paula? I'll bet you want your favorite—eggs sunnyside up, bacon, and pancakes. Right?"

My daddy took me to breakfast every single day. He let me order whatever I wanted, and just to make sure I was happy, he faithfully drew a smiley face on my pancakes with the syrup. It was our little joke.

I had to be the luckiest kid on earth because I was Daddy's little girl.

Next stop was the country club where Daddy and his friends—he called them "the boys"—laughed in smoke-filled rooms, drank heartily, played cards, and gambled. And as for little Paula? No, I didn't have to go to the children's day-care room. Instead, I was allowed to tear around, getting into anything and everything. That was OK, because everybody knew who I was: I was Daddy's little girl.

Some of my memories are clear, and some aren't, but I know that my mother worked, and worked hard. Mom owned a toy and craft store, and by midday of most days, Daddy and I went to see her. I'd run into the store and grab as many toys as I could hold in my arms. Mom always said *no*, but Daddy always grinned and said *yes!* I can still remember the anguish on her face, but it was years before I understood what it meant.

Once the visit with Mom was over, Daddy would call out, "Let's go, Paula!" We'd pile into the car, sometimes stopping at the park.

Eventually Daddy and I ended up back at the house where we turned on the TV, watched our favorite shows, and drank V-8 juice together. He'd stretch across the couch after a long day of playing with "the boys," and I'd cuddle next to him. I had to be the luckiest kid on earth because I was Daddy's little girl.

I still remember Daddy's broad shoulders. His long muscular legs made him seem as tall as a skyscraper. Daddy's hands were big, his smile was handsome, and his eyes were piercing. When I was with him, I felt so safe, so protected. Why? Because I was with *Superman*, of course. Whatever I needed or wanted, I knew that Superman would give it to me.

I still remember one particular day when my temperature suddenly shot up. This wasn't a normal childhood fever—the mercury rose so quickly that it broke the thermometer. My mother plunged me into a cool bath, but it didn't help. "We've got to get her to the hospital!" she shouted to my grandmother.

The emergency room was scary, and my little body was limp and lifeless. But Daddy was waiting there when we arrived, and he never left my side. His big hand was holding my tiny hand, and among the panicked voices, his strong voice was the only one I heard. "It's OK, Paula. Everything is going to be all right." I don't recall much else, but when I woke up I saw Daddy's face. I was going to be fine. Superman was there.

A few days later I woke up at about 2:00 A.M. I was hungry, and I demanded bacon. "We don't have any bacon," the nurse explained. "Besides, it's the middle of the night."

But I needn't have worried. Superman was there, and he would get me bacon. And he did. I knew that he would always give me whatever I wanted, because I was Daddy's little girl.

Once I got out of the hospital, we returned to our usual

routine—breakfast, the country club, and the toy store. Now and then, we went over to see Mama Annie, who was my great-grandmother. She was crippled with arthritis, and her body was terribly frail. Her back was humped over, and her hands were crooked and curled up. Her room smelled like a hospital, like alcohol and Ben-Gay, along with its own musty odor so intense that it caused me to hold my nose. But smell or no smell, I loved Mama Annie. She couldn't get around much, but she liked to rock me in her old, worn-out rocking chair. Holding me in her lap, she gently placed her crooked fingers on my head, and mumbled over me with great fervor and emotion. What was she saying? What was she doing? It was decades before I knew.

Moving On to Memphis

One evening, while I was staying with Mama Annie, it grew later and later. I wondered why Daddy hadn't come to get me. Where was he? Finally, Mom arrived instead. With a sigh and a weary expression on her face, she smiled at my great-grandma and said, "Thank you for watching her."

Young as I was, I noticed the pain in her eyes. When we got home, I jumped up on the couch where she was sitting. I wanted to comfort her, because by then tears were flowing down her cheeks.

"Mommy, why are you crying?"

Sobbing, she responded, "He took my milk money! I can't take this any longer! I can't believe he left me with nothing!"

I tried to understand her words. Couldn't take *what* any longer? Why was she crying? Where was my daddy?

It wasn't long before we packed everything we owned into boxes and suitcases, loaded up the car, and left Tupelo, Mississippi.

"Where are we going, Mom?" my brother asked.

"Memphis!" she responded.

It was in Memphis where we began our new life without Superman. And it was in Memphis—in that final, heartbreaking struggle between him and my mother—where I saw Daddy for the last time.

My little-girl reactions to Daddy's suicide are as clear to me today as they were the night of his death: *Will somebody please wake me up from this nightmare? This can't really be happening— or can it? Superman is not supposed to die! All I want is his big hands to embrace me, his long arms to hold me again and cuddle with me on the couch. All I want is to feel that place of refuge, safety, protection—all I want is to be loved!*

The next fourteen years became a search, a desperate journey during which I continued to ask, in a thousand different ways, "Will somebody please love me?" Surely Daddy's death had something to do with me. What could I have said differently? What could I have done to save his life?

Everyone had always told me that I was the apple of my Daddy's eye, but now two-plus-two wasn't adding up to four. *If he loved me so much, why did he leave me?* My little mind processed the fragments of information that were available and concluded that there must be something unlovable about me. There had to be something ugly in me. It must be true. Daddy was gone, and the evidence was growing every day.

"Why Am I Unlovable?"

One afternoon I ran through the neighborhood, excitedly handing out invitations to everyone I saw—young and old, boys and girls, even grandmothers. It was my first birthday after

Daddy's death, and he had always made my birthday a big celebration with balloons, a yellow cake with a twirling ballerina, and, of course, presents galore.

That year the celebration would be at 1:00 P.M. on my birthday. A ray of hope began to warm my heart. Maybe, just maybe, people would show up and celebrate how special I was. The big day arrived. I watched the hands of the clock move to 1:00 P.M., 1:15 P.M., then 1:30 P.M. My mother paced the floor. "Don't worry," she said. "They'll show up."

I heard a knock on the door. I ran, my heart pounding, and swung the door wide open. It was Anita, the little girl with freckles, stringy hair, and buckteeth. "H-a-a-p-p-y birthday," she stuttered; she handed me a small Hershey chocolate bar wrapped up in an old red hair ribbon.

That night I cried my eyes out. *Does anybody love me? Will somebody please love me?*

After my dad's death, our economic status changed drastically. My father had come from a family with money. After my father's death, his family took over the family business—leaving my mother without a place in the business. She was forced to seek other employment. My mother worked long, hard hours. I didn't see her much. There were always babysitters, often young girls and boys from the neighborhood. These sitters were older than I was, and they were supposed to protect me and watch over me. I trusted them as I had trusted Superman, but it wasn't long before the unthinkable happened.

One terrible day when I was just six years old, my childlike, boyish figure was violated. It would happen again and again in the weeks and years that followed. I ran and hid for hours after each occurrence. *I must be a bad girl,* I thought. I took long baths to try to wash away the dirtiness. As I sat in the bathtub, I would cry and silently plead with the world, *Does anybody love me? Will somebody please love me?*

Sometimes it seemed as if the whole world had turned against me. One special afternoon, I couldn't wait until the school bell

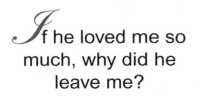

rang for dismissal. I couldn't do my classwork that day; I was too excited. Butterflies swarmed in my stomach. I continued looking at the clock every ten minutes, counting down. I had just joined my first Girl Scout Brownies troop, and we were going to take a field trip after school. It wasn't just any field trip—we were going to a television station to participate in the live audience for the *Bozo the Clown* program. We had to be at the school in our best outfits thirty minutes after school was dismissed.

By the time the bell rang, I could hardly breathe. I was ecstatic! I ran to my apartment just across the street. My best outfit? I knew exactly what to wear. I had just been given a brand new Hershey Park T-shirt, and I put it on with my favorite jeans and blue suede sneakers. I pulled my hair to the side and clipped the barrette. Looking in the mirror I thought, *Mom says my hair is always in my face, so I'll fix it pretty! Bozo, I'm going to look my best and be my best for you. I can't wait to play games on TV!*

I strutted out the door like a proud peacock and ran to the school. When I climbed on the bus, at first I didn't notice the bus mothers pointing and whispering. I was too excited about meeting Bozo. Then I began to look around and saw the other little girls had on dresses, lace, ribbons, and shiny shoes. Oh well, I reassured myself, no one had a brand new Hershey Park T-shirt like me!

When we finally arrived at the TV studio, they lined us up so we could be filmed entering the studio. I'd strategically found a seat in the front of the bus so I would be first in line. But suddenly a chaperoning mother roughly pulled me out of line and placed me at the back. I was disappointed and hurt, but I quickly got over it. The doors were opening, the noise was loud, and everything said, "Fun! This is going to be a great day."

We were seated in the studio, and I thought, *Let the games begin!* The production assistants started picking participants. I kept raising one hand, then both hands, then standing up, then shouting. Everyone on my bus was being chosen. I knew we would all get to play. Surely I was next. I couldn't believe it when the announcer walked across the stage and said it was over. What had happened? I boarded my bus. Every other girl in my troop had been chosen to play with Bozo except me. Why? I could not understand.

Again, I cried inside, *Does anybody love me? Will somebody please love me?*

My mind quickly computed the evidence, and the verdict was coming out quite clearly: *Paula, you are unlovable.*

But I wasn't so easily defeated. *I know how I can fix that,* I thought. *I'll cover it up and no one will ever see it.* So, brick by brick I unconsciously began to build a wall around myself. It would be years before I understood that the walls we build in our lives to keep intruders out are the same walls that keep us imprisoned inside. My own particular "Alcatraz" turned into an impenetrable prison.

Trying to Be Perfect

I reasoned: *If you cannot love me for who I am, I will become what you love. Surely you will love a good girl, a straight-A student, an athlete, a hard worker, a pretty girl, a skinny girl—surely you can love that person. So I will become her.* I had no idea that I was embarking on a self-destructive journey, one that would take away what little identity I did have, one that would leave me wondering who Paula really was.

I strove diligently for "perfection." I took my report card and showed it to anyone and everyone who would give me two seconds of their time. I made sure they saw the straight As (with an occasional B) that I had earned. I flashed my grades before my teachers each time I entered a new classroom. I sent a copy of my report card to every address I had. I flaunted my accomplishments to my mother and family. *Aren't you proud of me? Don't you love me?*

But grades weren't enough. With a natural knack to do cartwheels and somersaults, I decided to become a top competitive gymnast. After all, everyone loved the gymnasts: They "ooh-ed" and "aah-ed" over their natural ease and ability to twist and turn while flying through the air. I was a late beginner, signing up for classes just prior to junior high school. But that did not deter me, because everyone loved a gymnast.

One week into classes, I learned that in order to advance to the intermediate level of competition, I had to do a back handspring during the floor exercises. I was determined to make the team and bring home the medals. So I set the alarm clock for 5:00 A.M. The instant I heard it buzz, I jumped out of bed, grabbed my blue-and-white checkered Snoopy sleeping bag, and rushed to the damp, cold grass outside. It was still dark.

I doubled the sleeping bag to create a makeshift mat. Then I began the process. Hands in front of me, body positioned as if I were sitting in an invisible chair, I thrust my arms over my head in a backward motion and ordered my body to follow. Over and over again, crashing on my head, landing sideways, feet flying in the air, arms giving out under the weight of my body, I continued to practice. I was determined. Then it happened! On the sixth day I did a perfect back handspring, just as I had seen it done on TV and in the gym. It was an impeccable demonstration of strength and grace. I had mastered a very difficult move, and I advanced.

Inside I was still crying, *Aren't you proud of me? Don't you love me? Won't somebody please love me?*

Even success at gymnastics wasn't enough to fill my need for approval. I had fine limp brown hair, beady little brown eyes, chipmunk cheeks. And to make matters worse, my figure wasn't at all the way I wanted it to be. While everyone else was testing their body fat by "pinching an inch," I figured there was at least a good foot or so of fat to grab on me.

I went to a party my junior year in high school. The sign posted in the front yard read "NO FAT CHICKS." Billboards, television, magazines, friends, family, strangers, and acquaintances all proclaimed the same message, explicitly or implicitly: "To be thin is to be beautiful...to be beautiful is to be loved."

Looking around campus, I compared myself to some of the other students. There was one girl in particular who caught my attention. "Isn't she pretty? Look how beautiful she is!" everyone exclaimed as she walked down the school hall. "What a turn-around from last year! She was so big, so fat! No one even knew her name before, and now she's our new 'Miss Popularity.'"

"But how did she do it?" I inquired. "What's her secret?"

"Easy," someone told me. "She purges!"

"Purges? What's that?"

"You know. She throws up after she eats."

"Incredible! It's that easy?"

So I began to purge myself after each meal. But it wasn't enough. *I can do better,* I told myself, *because to be thin is to be beautiful, and to be beautiful is to be loved. I will not only purge myself, but I will stop eating. I will exercise. I will be thinner than anyone!*

My weight began to drop rapidly. I purged myself even if I drank a glass of juice. My menstrual cycles ceased. My body grew weak. But I was undeniably thin!

Aren't you proud of how I look? Don't you love me? Won't somebody please love me? For seven years I struggled with eating disorders.

The Hunt for a Hero

In the midst of so many futile efforts to find the love I longed for, my pain turned to denial. I began to imagine that my Superman, my hero, had not really died. After all, heroes are immortal. Heroes live forever. I tried to convince myself that my Superman would come back. But he didn't.

My denial soon turned to anger. I was angry at my mother for marrying my father. I was angry at the people who were supposed to protect me and had abused me instead. I was angry at the world. My heart became callous. I no longer cried, "Somebody, please love me!" I no longer cried at all.

My anger turned into manipulation: I began to manipulate every relationship in my life. If my mother tried to correct me, I knew how to shut her up instantly: "But you don't know what it's like! Your dad didn't kill himself!" Whether it was a friend, a teacher, or a potential new "hero," I did the same thing. I was beginning to discover that manipulation gave me the ability to control other people, or at least I thought it did.

Meanwhile, I continued to search for "Superman" candidates, for a man who could fill the void that the loss of my daddy had left in my heart. I was looking for someone who would understand me, value me, and appreciate me. I was determined to find someone who would love me. Even though, apparently, there was something in me that was unlovable, I continued my hunt for a hero.

During my junior year in high school I attended a dance. I was getting a drink of water when suddenly I felt a tap on my shoulder. I turned around and there he was—my hero! Light brown hair, deep, dark eyes, olive skin, and a big beautiful smile. I was soon to discover that he also had a witty personality.

"Do you want to dance?" he asked.

Without hesitation, I smiled, "Yeah."

I'd been waiting for this moment. One dance led to another. He asked if I wanted to go out the following weekend, and of course I said *yes* to that, too. The dance led to a date, and one date led to another, and a relationship began to develop. He bought me presents, picked me up for school each morning, and talked to me for hours.

Sometimes I questioned myself: *Is this it? Is this love?* For some reason, I still had that dissatisfaction inside, that void and emptiness. Maybe physical intimacy would fill it. I allowed a physical relationship to develop. *Is this it?* I asked myself after my first physical encounter. *Is this love? Is this as good as it gets?* The hollowness in the pit of my stomach grew deeper. Now I not only felt void and empty, I felt vulnerable and empty. *Maybe I picked the wrong candidate for my hero,* I thought. *I'll try a different one.*

I developed a behavior pattern. One young man followed another, and in every case, at the moment when I began to feel vulnerable, I'd push him out. I had unconsciously determined,

You will not leave me, abandon me, or reject me. I will not give you the opportunity!

Then I began to consider another option. *Maybe if I get married, that will be the solution to my emptiness.*

He wasn't exactly a hero. He wasn't Superman, either. But he was a rock-and-roll singer, and what stage presence he had! We barely knew each other; however, I was quite sure that a marriage license and a ring would constitute intimacy and commitment. We both entered the relationship with more excess baggage than we could have possibly known.

I thought saying "I do" would make everything great. Little did I know that marriage would only be a magnifying glass for pre-existing conditions. It was as if I had been put under a microscope, and all the problems, all the insecurities, and all the hang-ups had been enlarged. The brief marriage ended. I was devastated. Could I ever be loved, valued, appreciated, made whole, fixed, complete, and mended? Would the emptiness ever cease? Would the void ever be filled?

An Unexpected Meeting

One afternoon, I was in the trailer home of an older woman. Her middle-aged son was visiting from several states away. I was sitting at her little round kitchenette table, and we were talking about all kinds of things. All at once he abruptly asked me, "Aren't you tired of your life? Don't you want to know real love?"

Didn't I want to know real love? Of course I did, but how could he have known? By then I had become a master disguise artist. I had dressed up my pain, fixed my hair on top of it, learned to square my shoulders back, and to sit up straight and tall. And surely my ear-to-ear smile should have thrown him off. So how did he know?

My heart began to pound. Would I keep on pretending everything was OK forever while I was dying inside? Unexplainably, I felt a sudden calm. I had no idea why, but for a moment all the confusion stopped, and all the walls tumbled down. Somehow I felt like the little girl who had once trusted, who had once hoped. I felt a strange sense of safety.

I could hardly believe it when I heard myself reply, "Yes, I'm tired of my life, and I want to know real love."

The man pulled out a book. On its front cover two words were printed: "Holy Bible." He began to read. "For God so loved the world, that he gave his only begotten Son, that whosoever believeth in him should not perish, but have everlasting life" (John 3:16).

This is incredible! Yes, I want real love! Yes, I want my life changed! Yes, I want You, Jesus, as my personal Savior!

He explained to me that Jesus Christ is the Son of God (Matt. 27:54; John 20:31). He told me that the entire human race had become sinful and separated from God (Rom. 3:23; 5:12). But because God loved men and women so much, He sent His only Son to pay the price of redemption so that people could be reconciled to God again (Rom. 5:10; 2 Cor. 5:18).

The man explained how Jesus had walked the earth almost two thousand years ago and had gone to an old rugged cross called Calvary to pay the ultimate price. Jesus had given His life and shed His blood to redeem mankind (1 John 1:7). He was buried in a borrowed tomb (Matt. 27:60). He descended to hell and took the keys to death, hell, and the grave (Eph. 4:9; Matt. 12:40; Rev. 1:18). On the third day He rose again (Luke 18:33; 1 Cor. 15:4). He ascended to heaven, redeeming mankind back to God (Mark 16:19; Eph. 4:9).

My friend's son told me how Jesus had done this so I would not have to live in defeat. Jesus had come to give me life more abundantly (John 10:10). Jesus wanted to set me free from all of my bondage, self-deception, and insecurity (Luke 4:18; John 8:32, 36).

He told me that if I would confess with my mouth and believe in my heart that God had raised Jesus from the dead, I would be saved (Rom. 10:9-10).

Saved? What did *saved* mean? It could only mean that I was about to be rescued from destruction and placed in safety. Oh, what a marvelous thought. It was wonderful! I had heard the name of Jesus before, but only used as profanity or in the same context as the Tooth Fairy or Santa Claus. I did not know that Jesus Christ was the Son of God. And I could never have imagined that Jesus actually loved me—loved me so much that He gave His life so that I could be reconciled to God. I would never have thought that I would someday cry out, "Abba, Father," which was another way of saying "Daddy" (Rom. 8:15).

My response was nothing short of ecstatic. "This is incredible! Yes, I want real love! Yes, I want my life changed! Yes, I want You, Jesus, as my personal Savior!"

The man gently grabbed my hands and asked me to repeat a prayer of salvation. Afterward, I felt as if a thousand pounds had been lifted off my heart. The feeling was different from anything I had ever experienced. I was so light inside. That "dark hole" in the middle of my stomach was disappearing. The void, the emptiness had been filled. For the first time since the death of my daddy, I felt love (1 John 4:16). Paula wasn't unlovable after all!

It was the most glorious day of my life. I had accepted Jesus Christ, the living Son of God, as my personal Lord and Savior. The man who made this marvelous introduction in my life had to return to his home, but he gave me a Bible and instructed me to find a church and to read the Bible daily. I began to do so. I knew I was different. There had been a drastic change in my life—I was saved. I was rescued. Most of all, *I was loved.*

Personal Reflections

Think About This

Read the quotes from this chapter below. After each one take a moment to reflect on how the statement links to a feeling or experience in your own life. Give your own personal reaction to each statement.

1. The next fourteen years became a search, a desperate journey during which I continued to ask, in a thousand different ways, "Will somebody please love me?" The author is describing her desperate search to find love. What are the ways that you have used in an attempt to find love? Did they work?

_____

_____

_____

_____

_____

2. I reasoned: *If you cannot love me for who I am, I will become what you love. Surely you will love a good girl, a straight-A student, an athlete, a hard worker, a pretty girl, a skinny girl—surely you can love that person. So I will become her.* I had no idea that I was

embarking on a self-destructive journey. The author thought perfection could bring love to her. Have you ever tried to find love in this way? Describe your experience:

_____

_____

_____

_____

_____

_____

3. My friend's son told me…that if I would confess with my mouth and believe in my heart that God had raised Jesus from the dead, I would be saved (Rom. 10:9–10). My response was nothing short of ecstatic. "This is incredible! Yes, I want real love! Yes, I want my life changed! Yes, I want You, Jesus, as my personal Savior!" The man gently grabbed my hands and asked me to repeat a prayer of salvation. Afterward, I felt as if a thousand pounds had been lifted off my heart.

The author describes the moment when she encountered God's love and salvation for the first time.

Describe your own encounter with the love of God.

Maybe you've never responded to the love of God. If you've never accepted Jesus Christ as your personal Savior, why don't you take the next few minutes and, in your own words, ask Him to come into your heart and change your life forever.

Talk to God

Lord, thank You for interrupting my life and for revealing Yourself and Your love to me. Thank You for dying on the cross for my sins and making it possible for me to receive You into my life as my Lord and Savior. Before I knew You, I could not see my destiny, the big picture of the life You had planned for me, because of the clouds of hurt and rejection that filled my mind and heart. But You loved me all along, and although I could not see it at the time, when my father died, You stepped in and became my Daddy. Thank You for doing what no one else could do. You went to the inner part of my heart where no one else could touch me. Thank You for loving me, even though I believed I was unlovable. Amen.

THREE

Right Heart, Wrong Head

Without knowledge of the truth, we cannot be free. In His Word, God declares, "*My people* are destroyed for lack of knowledge" (Hos. 4:6). He wasn't speaking to the heathen. He wasn't speaking to unrepentant sinners. God said, "My people are destroyed for lack of knowledge."

I believe it is possible for us to have a right heart for God and yet to have things all wrong in our heads. And with a wrong head, we may very well live in complete defeat and lose ground in the kingdom of God. This has nothing to do with our hearts or with our worship. Our lives can be destroyed because of ignorance. We are sometimes ignorant of the truth, and until we learn it, we remain in bondage to our old ways. Jesus said, "And ye shall know the truth, and the truth shall make you free" (John 8:32). I had to learn this important lesson myself, and I learned it the hard way—by experience.

A Man Named Randy

During the first few years of my Christian walk I made some of the biggest mistakes of my life. I found out that old habits die hard—old habits like manipulation, control games, and well-worn ways of thinking that had been deeply ingrained in me from the past. I struggled with the tension between my head and my heart. Something was definitely new and different on the inside, but my outward behavior did not always project this change. I still *thought* the same as I had before, prior to my salvation experience, which in turn made me *act* in many of the same ways.

The difference with my behavior was that now my actions did not *feel* right. This condition is sometimes called *conviction*, but I would not understand what it was or from whom it came for many years. I ignored many of conviction's warning signs and signals. I was unable to recognize that the source of my discomfort was actually God in the person of the Holy Spirit, living inside me and trying to guide and instruct me.

The New Testament declares, "Know ye not that ye are the temple of God, and that the Spirit of God dwelleth in you?" (1 Cor. 3:16). In fact, I had no idea about the indwelling of the Holy Spirit. But God wanted me to know, and He knew how to get my attention.

His name was Randy. I met him in a Maryland church—he was tall, had blonde hair, blue eyes, and was a little pudgy at the time. He was unlike anyone I had ever dated before. I had usually sought out the tall, dark, handsome type of man.

Randy and I first went out for a business lunch and continued to see each other from that time on. As months passed the friendship began to develop into a relationship, and I found myself falling in love with him. Of course, the usual voices inside my head tried to caution me, "Oh no, Paula! You'd better be careful. What if he gets to know the *real* you? What if he looks behind the walls? He'll see that there's something unlovable in you, and then he'll leave you, hurt you, reject you, and abandon you." As yet, I did not see myself as God saw me, so I could not understand that I was lovable.

In any case, our relationship began to get serious. One Friday night our conversation led to a heated discussion, which, in turn, led to an all-out argument. I was losing ground, so all my defenses rose up, trying to lock me safely inside. I was in danger! I was being exposed!

I reacted quickly. I knew exactly what to do. Manipulation had always worked before. So I fell to the ground, pulled my knees to my chest, and curled myself into a fetal position. The crocodile tears began to flow. My breathing got heavy, and I knew I could even hyperventilate if necessary. My speech was interrupted by great gasps of heaving sobs. I screamed out my well-rehearsed lines: "You don't know! You don't understand! Your daddy didn't kill himself. You weren't abused."

I put my head down to my chest and closed my eyes, knowing that at any moment Randy's strong arms would wrap around me and comfort me. He would bend down and hold me; he would sympathize and make all the wrong go away.

A minute passed, then two minutes. Why was I not feeling his touch? I opened one eye and slightly lifted my head from my fetal position in curiosity. Why wasn't he rescuing me yet? Randy was standing there staring at me with a stern look on his face. I lifted my head higher. Both eyes were now open and staring at him, silently pleading with him for a reaction.

His words weren't the ones I expected to hear. "When you

want to act like an adult and talk to me," he said coolly, "then we will talk." With that he turned and strode out of the building.

I could not believe it! How could my most foolproof method of manipulation not be working? I began to cry louder, even hysterically. Surely he would listen and run back to me! Louder and louder I wailed until the whole community could have heard me. But it was all to no avail—Randy was gone.

Eventually I pulled myself to my feet, wiped my face, and began to pace the floor. Now I was angry. How could he be so unsympathetic? So cold? I tried to convince myself that he would surely call me later that night. Or maybe he would stop by. After all, we talked at least five times a day and had dinner together almost every night. I sat by the phone knowing it would ring at any moment. But it didn't.

A day passed, then two days. Three, four, five, ten days—and not a word. I have a stubborn streak in me. *I won't give in!* I thought. Eleven, twelve, fourteen days. After two endless weeks, I stood in my bedroom and looked in the mirror. Other than checking out my appearance, I'm not sure I had ever really looked at myself before, at least not quite like that. I stared for what seemed to be hours. I took a good, long look. What exactly was the problem here? Could it be that the problem was staring me back in the face?

I picked up the phone and called Randy. He answered, "Oh, I see you're ready to act like an adult," he said pleasantly. "Now we can work through this."

For the first time in my life someone was willing to confront the manipulative routine I had used throughout my life to get my way. Randy did not judge me, nor did he conclude that my character was hopelessly flawed. But he wasn't about to give in to my ploys. Today Randy is my wonderful husband. He has truly been sent as the iron to sharpen iron in my life (Prov. 27:17). I can never thank God enough for him.

"Show Me the Answers!"

After that incident, I concluded (very wisely) that there would have to be a change in my behavior, and the sooner the better.

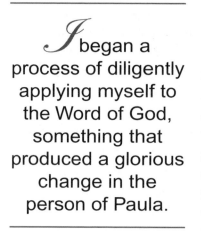

I began a process of diligently applying myself to the Word of God, something that produced a glorious change in the person of Paula.

But how and where should I start? One night, while walking through my bedroom, I impulsively picked up the Bible. I had tried to read it from the day I first accepted the Lord, but most of it had made no sense to me. I didn't realize at the time that the Bible was written to my spirit self, not to my natural self or my natural mind. Scripture is inspired by the Spirit of God to be understood spiritually, and the Holy Spirit would have to reveal the Word of God to me, giving me the understanding I needed to produce permanent change in my life.

That night I held the Bible up and declared, "Lord, I don't want to be fifty and still all messed up! I don't want to be circling the same mountain then that I'm circling now. I don't want to be on my fourth or fifth marriage and still confused! I have so many questions, and I believe the answers are in this book, the Bible. I will study it. Would You please show me the answers?"

From that time on, I began a process of diligently applying myself to the Word of God, something that produced a glorious change in the person of Paula. Today, that process continues. Just when I think I have the victory in one area, God reveals another area in which I need to grow. God's Word explains:

> But we all, with open face beholding as in a glass the glory of the Lord, are changed into the same image from glory to glory, even as by the Spirit of the Lord.
> —2 CORINTHIANS 3:18

In the years since that first encounter with God's Word, I've learned that spiritual growth is a continual work between the Holy Spirit and us. The more we press into the things of God, the more our flesh, our outward character must die. The apostle Paul wrote, "And they that are Christ's have crucified the flesh with the affections and lusts" (Gal. 5:24).

He also said, "I am crucified with Christ: nevertheless I live; yet not I, but Christ liveth in me: and the life which I now live in the flesh I live by the faith of the Son of God, who loved me, and gave himself for me" (Gal. 2:20). In another passage, we read, "For though we walk in the flesh, we do not war after the flesh...For the weapons of our warfare are not carnal, but mighty through God to the pulling down of strong holds" (2 Cor. 10:3–4).

Once we understand that we do not war according to the flesh, half of our battle is won. We cannot escape our flesh—we live in the flesh. As long as I am in this natural body I will have to deal with my flesh and the works of it. However I do not *war* in the flesh. That means that even though I am living in this fleshly body I cannot operate with fleshly tactics such as temper, jealousy, anger, and other manipulative emotions.

So, how do we live in the flesh but not be led by our flesh? Paul tells us how in Romans 8:5: "For they that are after the flesh do mind the things of the flesh; but they that are after the Spirit the things of the Spirit." If I do want to be led by my spirit rather than by my flesh, then I must keep in mind the things of the Spirit.

Transformation and Renewal

The key to transformation in my life is to walk in the Spirit and not in the flesh. How do I do that? In Romans 12:2 we are instructed, "And be not conformed to this world: but be ye transformed by the renewing of your mind, that ye may prove what is that good, and acceptable, and perfect, will of God."

There are four key words that we need to dissect and understand:

1. *Conformed*—from the Greek word *suschematizo*, meaning "to conform to another's example; to mimic or imitate."

2. *World*—from the Greek word *aion*, meaning "age or times."

3. *Transformed*—from the Greek word *metamorphoo*, meaning "transformed or transfigured by a supernatural change."

4. *Prove*—from the Greek word *dokimazo*, meaning "allow, discern, and examine."

In more familiar words, we are not to pattern ourselves after this age or according to the times. Instead, we are to be transfigured like a caterpillar to a butterfly. How? By the renewing of our mind, so that we are able to allow, discern, and examine what is the good, acceptable, and perfect will of God!

People often ask: "How can I know the perfect will of God for my life?" According to the Word of God, we are transformed and changed by the renewing of our mind *into the perfect will of God.* To really understand this and to walk in it, let's look at it more closely. We are made up of three basic parts: spirit, soul, and body. "And the very God of peace sanctify you wholly; and I pray God your whole spirit and soul and body be preserved blameless unto the coming of our Lord Jesus Christ" (1 Thess. 5:23).

Our body is the most insignificant part of ourselves. It simply houses our soul and spirit. It will one day return to dust from where it came, to be resurrected only when Jesus returns. Yet the body seems to be the area where we make the greatest investment of time and energy. Most people spend more time, money, and energy on their bodies and their fleshly desires than on the unseen aspects of themselves.

Now there is nothing wrong with taking care of the "packaging," as long as we do not neglect the gift inside. I encourage you to take care of your temple—it is the house of God's Spirit! We have to realize and understand the body's significance. Anything gained in the flesh will have to be maintained in the flesh.

Besides the body, we need to consider the soul. Our soul encompasses our mind, will, and emotions. It is the seat of our passions.

We also need to understand our human spirit, which is our immortal, innermost being. The spirit is the part of us that is able to be born again. We learn about this in the story of Nicodemus, found in John 3:1–6:

> There was a man of the Pharisees, named Nicodemus, a ruler of the Jews: The same came to Jesus by night, and said unto him, Rabbi, we know that thou art a teacher come from God: for no man can do these miracles that thou doest, except God be with him.

> Jesus answered and said unto him, Verily, verily, I say unto thee, Except a man be born again, he cannot see the kingdom of God.
>
> Nicodemus saith unto him, How can a man be born when he is old? Can he enter the second time into his mother's womb, and be born?
>
> Jesus answered, Verily, verily, I say unto thee, Except a man be born of water and of the Spirit, he cannot enter into the kingdom of God. That which is born of the flesh is flesh; and that which is born of the Spirit is spirit.

When we are saved or become born again, our human spirit man does a 180-degree turn.

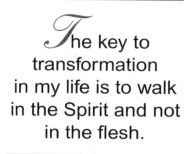

The key to transformation in my life is to walk in the Spirit and not in the flesh.

We were in darkness, but now we are in the light. "But ye are a chosen generation, a royal priesthood, an holy nation, a peculiar people; that ye should shew forth the praises of him who hath called you out of darkness into his marvellous light" (1 Pet. 2:9).

Once our spirit is born again, we are on our way to heaven: "For the wages of sin is death; but the gift of God is eternal life through Jesus Christ our Lord" (Rom. 6:23).

When we are born again, our names are written in the Lamb's Book of Life: "He that overcometh, the same shall be clothed in white raiment; and I will not blot out his name out of the book of life, but I will confess his name before my Father, and before his angels" (Rev. 3:5).

However, my body and my mind aren't born again or saved. So I look and think the same way as I did before I got saved. This, in turn, makes me act in the same way I did before. Have you ever heard the old saying, "I sold my soul to the devil"? The devil really does want our soul, mind, will, and emotions. He wants it because our soul is the hinge that swings the door. My soul will determine my direction, whether I am going to walk in the Spirit or in the flesh. That is why God instructed us in the Word to be trans-formed, changed, transfigured by the renewing of our mind. The word *renewing* means "renovation."

A New Way of Thinking

We once did a home renovation, and it was quite a process. We had to repair, restore, take away the old, and make new. God's Word says that we are changed by the renewing or renovation of our mind (Rom. 12:2). The Holy Spirit is the foreman of the construction site, and the Word of God is the tool that is used for the process.

I cannot overemphasize this enough: Jesus said, "Heaven and earth shall pass away, but my words shall not pass away" (Matt. 24:35). If my thoughts, philosophies, ideas, or reasoning are built on anything but the Word of God, they are nothing but sinking sand. They will not last; they will not produce the promises God has guaranteed me in His Word. I must get rid of my old ways of thinking. I must build a new thought process based on the Word of God.

The apostle Paul instructed his protégé Timothy in 2 Timothy 2:15: "Study to shew thyself approved unto God, a workman that needeth not to be ashamed, rightly dividing the word of truth." In the final analysis, whatever my mother has told me—whatever my teachers, my doctors, my friends, my family, or even my pastor says—is not going to matter unless it is in alignment and agreement with the Word of God. God's Word produces God's promises. The

Lord has proclaimed through the prophet Isaiah, "So shall my word be that goeth forth out of my mouth: it shall not return unto me void, but it shall accomplish that which I please, and it shall prosper in the thing whereto I sent it" (Isa. 55:11).

When my confrontation with Randy caused me to stop and examine my life as a born-again believer, I soon realized that my behavior was not lining up with God's Word. Of course, I quickly concluded that the problem was not God's but mine.

Jesus stated in John 10:10: "I am come that they might have life, and that they might have it more abundantly." I like the Amplified Version, which states: "I came that they may have and enjoy life, and have it in abundance (to the full, till it overflows)." God wanted me to have abundant life, but I didn't have it. What was wrong?

Initially I kept thinking, *If I just have more faith, then surely I will see God's promises manifested in my life.* Then I learned that my concept of faith was wrong. I treated faith like hopeful wishing. What most people call faith is not faith at all; it is high expectation based on wrong information. True faith is synonymous with the Word of God. In fact, faith *is* the Word of God: no Word, no faith.

There are two systems in operation all around us: the world's system and God's system—the kingdom of God.

Seeking God's Kingdom

Everything operates with the world's system or God's system, which we call His kingdom. Our marriages, our relationships, our careers, our ministries, our finances—all these are operating in one system or the other.

Jesus said, "But seek ye first the kingdom of God, and his righteousness; and all these things shall be added unto you" (Matt. 6:33). If we want "all these things"—the promises of

God—added to our life, then we have to seek the kingdom of God *first*. That is not as easily done as said, because *seeking*, in itself, can be very frustrating. Nobody seeks just for the sake of seeking. There must be a good deal of desperation to push us through the seeking process.

Only when we become desperate enough to endure the struggle and overcome the obstacles will we find what we seek. That is why it is not enough for us to like God or want God—we must desperately *need* God.

When I finally faced the fact that I couldn't continue to live in the same old manipulative ways, I said, "God, if You don't change me, I cannot live victoriously!"

When my eyes said, "Stop reading the Word! You need to go to sleep," I responded, "I *need* God!"

When my ears said, "Not another tape!" I responded, "I *need* God!"

When my body said, "You've been sitting too long—not another Christian speaker!" I responded, "I *need* God!"

My desperation enabled me to press through the seeking process.

But once we are determined to seek, what is it that we are seeking? "Seek ye first the kingdom of God." But what is the kingdom of God? Let's look at the word *kingdom*. *Kingdom* means "the dominion is of the king." So the "kingdom of God" refers to the way the King operates His system. Simply put, it is God's way of doing things. If we want the promises of God released in our lives, then we must understand God's way of doing things.

Let's consider Mark 4:26–29:

> And he said, So is the kingdom of God, as if a man
> should cast seed into the ground; and should sleep,

and rise night and day, and the seed should spring and grow up, he knoweth not how. For the earth bringeth forth fruit of herself; first the blade, then the ear, after that the full corn in the ear. But when the fruit is brought forth, immediately he putteth in the sickle, because the harvest is come.

You do not plant corn today and eat corn tomorrow. There is a growth process that must take place. You can't wait until your life is a mess to begin planting the Word of God and then expect immediate results. Growth doesn't happen overnight; it occurs gradually. Plant the Word of God now to bring His promised results and harvest into your future.

> *O*nly when we become desperate enough to endure the struggle and overcome the obstacles will we find what we seek.

How do you plant the Word of God? The Word of God does no good in your notebook or lying on a shelf somewhere. The kingdom of God requires you to plant seeds; there are sixty-six books in the Bible, every one of them full of seeds. How do you plant to produce the promises or harvest of God in your life? *You take the Word of God out of the Bible and plant it in your heart.* The human heart is the ground for planting the Word of God.

How do I get the seed out of the Bible and into my heart? There are three entrances to the heart:

- Mouth gate
- Eye gate
- Ear gate

I plant the Word of God through what I say, what I see, and what I hear, and it produces my thought life. My thought life, in turn, determines my behavior. That is why Paul wrote:

> Finally, brethren, whatsoever things are true, whatsoever things are honest, whatsoever things are just, whatsoever things are pure, whatsoever things are lovely, whatsoever things are of good report; if there be any virtue, and if there be any praise, think on these things. Those things, which ye have both learned, and received, and heard, and seen in me, do: and the God of peace shall be with you.
> —PHILIPPIANS 4:8–9

Thoughts become words...

Words become actions...

Actions become habits...

Habits become character...

Character becomes destiny.

As I learned so many years ago, being born again will give you the right heart for eternal life. But until your mind is renewed, you'll have the wrong head. And with the wrong head, you will live a defeated life. Only by living in the truth of God's Word can you fully enter into the kingdom of God.

Personal Reflections

Think About This

Read the quotes from this chapter below. After each one take a moment to reflect on how the statement links to a feeling or experience in your own life. Give your own personal reaction to each statement.

1. For the first time in my life someone was willing to confront the manipulative routine I had used throughout my life to get my way. Randy did not judge me, nor did he conclude that my character was hopelessly flawed. But he wasn't about to give in to my ploys. Today Randy is my wonderful husband. He has truly been sent as the iron to sharpen iron in my life (Prov. 27:17). I can never thank God enough for him.

In the paragraph above, the author describes how God used her husband to help her overcome using negative tactics to gain love. Who are the individuals in your life whom God has used to help you grow spiritually?

_____

_____

_____

_____

2. In the years since that first encounter with God's Word, I've learned that spiritual growth is a continual work between the Holy Spirit and us. The more we press into the things of God, the more our flesh, our outward character must die. List the ways that you are attempting to "press into the things of God." How is the Holy Spirit using God's Word to effect spiritual growth in your life?

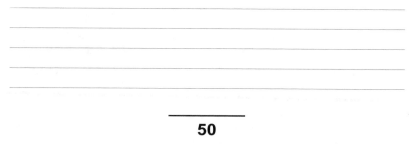

3. You do not plant corn today and eat corn tomorrow. There is a growth process that must take place. You can't wait until your life is a mess to begin planting the Word of God and then expect immediate results. Growth doesn't happen overnight; it occurs gradually. Plant the Word of God now to bring His promised results and harvest into your future. List at least three Scripture verses to which you will commit, allowing the principles from these verses to change your life. Tell what change you want each verse to help you make.

Talk to God

> *Lord, expose to me everything in my life that is contrary to Your Word or Your will. Destroy every thought, every philosophy that is not in agreement with You. For it is Your Word alone that will produce life in me. Although I love You, I recognize that I can go down the wrong road because I lack knowledge. Give me a hunger and thirst for Your Word. Holy Spirit, reveal to me the Word of the Lord and give me the mind of Christ. Amen.*

FOUR

Who God Isn't

Even after I was born again, I really wasn't free from my past. I lived like a person who was always expecting something to go wrong, waiting for the other shoe to drop, behaving emotionally like someone who would have to face punishment for all the bad things she had done in her life. Even though I knew that I had been spared the final judgment of hell, I still felt that surely I owed God some kind of restitution.

I assumed that God was just waiting for the moment when I would mess up, and then *Bam!* That would be it. I guess, unconsciously, I pictured God as the sheriff—complete with badge, nightstick, and whipping post. In my mind, He was ready to strike and was eagerly awaiting my failure.

How absolutely wrong I was! Why? Not because I didn't deserve punishment, but because I had a false concept of God. And why did I have this concept of God?

Because I viewed God in the same way I viewed people. My concept of love was that if I could somehow manage to be "good enough," someone would love me. I had always believed that love had to be earned, deserved, and was conditional upon my behavior. After all, isn't that what most of us are taught?

Understanding God's Love

> For this cause I bow my knees unto the Father of our Lord Jesus Christ, of whom the whole family in heaven and earth is named, that he would grant you, according to the riches of his glory, to be strengthened with might by his Spirit in the inner man; that Christ may dwell in your hearts by faith; that ye, being rooted and grounded in love, may be able to comprehend with all saints what is the breadth, and length, and depth, and height; and to know the love of Christ, which passeth knowledge, that ye might be filled with all the fulness of God.
>
> —EPHESIANS 3:14–19

In this prayer, the apostle Paul reflects that if we could understand the love of God, we would be filled with the fullness of God. Paul knew that there are many people who serve God but who do not know Him or understand His love.

God's Word says, "There is therefore now no condemnation to them which are in Christ Jesus, who walk not after the flesh, but after the Spirit" (Rom. 8:1). There is no guilty verdict, no sentence upon me when I walk in the Spirit and not in the flesh. God is not sitting in judgment of me, because He has already judged Jesus for my sins. But for years and years, that is not the way I felt or lived.

As a little girl, I remember being scolded and told repeatedly, "You are a bad girl." Naturally, after I was saved, I figured that I was still a bad girl. In fact, in some ways I felt worse than ever, because I now knew right from wrong.

Life conditions us to focus on the negatives in our lives. My school tests would come back marked 97 percent—a good solid A. But the questions I had answered properly were not marked with ninety-seven bright, yellow happy faces next to them. Instead, there were three huge red check marks next to the ones I had missed. This, of course, pointed out to me my failures and inadequacies. God was the greatest Teacher of all. Shouldn't I expect the same red check marks from Him?

No, God isn't just another human teacher. His Word says that we cannot even begin to think the way He does.

> For my thoughts are not your thoughts, neither are your ways my ways, saith the LORD. For as the heavens are higher than the earth, so are my ways higher than your ways, and my thoughts than your thoughts.
> —ISAIAH 55:8–9

However, even though the Scriptures contradicted the way I felt, it took me a long time to understand that God is not like people, or at least like the way I perceived people to be. I had the most difficult time with this. How could I accept love from a God whom I could not see and could not touch? I had not yet even learned to receive love from people whom I *could* see and *could* touch.

Learning to Say "Abba, Father!"

The more I studied the Word of God, the more I was able to see that God is not on the judgment seat. Our heavenly Father is in the family den, ready to open His arms and receive us as His beloved children.

> For as many as are led by the Spirit of God, they are
> the sons of God. For ye have not received the spirit of
> bondage again to fear; but ye have received the Spirit
> of adoption, whereby we cry, Abba, Father. The Spirit
> itself beareth witness with our spirit, that we are the
> children of God.
>
> —ROMANS 8:14–16

I can come to God through His Son, Jesus Christ, and He will welcome me as my Daddy! But how can I cry "Abba, Father," which is another way of saying "Daddy," if I never had a trustworthy father? What reference point do I have to go by? How can I crawl up in His lap and rest in His bosom and know that He will not leave me, abandon me, or reject me? How do I know that He will not hurt me the way other people whom I trusted did, people who were supposed to protect me and watch out for my well-being and best interests?

It was many years after I first received Jesus Christ as my Savior before I was able to understand my destiny in Him. In Jeremiah 1:5 we read, "Before I formed thee in the belly I knew thee; and before thou camest forth out of the womb I sanctified thee." I did not comprehend the concept that before I was ever a twinkle in my daddy's eye or a thought in my mother's mind, God knew me and had already set me apart. I did not realize that all the junk that happened in my life was intended to distract, disrupt, and ruin the most significant relationship I would ever know—my relationship with God. I could not discern that there had been "assignments" sent into my life by the enemy of God to mess up forever the reason for my existence, which is to commune and have fellowship with God.

Only through God's Word and through the ministry of godly

people, and especially my husband, Randy, did I ever begin to see just how much God loves me. God says to all of us, "Yea, I have loved thee with an everlasting love: therefore with lovingkindness have I drawn thee" (Jer. 31:3). If only we believed it!

Living Like "Dogs"

There is a story in 2 Samuel about a young man named Mephibosheth that makes me think about those of us who simply don't have a good understanding of God's love.

> And Jonathan, Saul's son, had a son that was lame of his feet. He was five years old when the tidings came of Saul and Jonathan out of Jezreel, and his nurse took him up, and fled: and it came to pass, as she made haste to flee, that he fell, and became lame. And his name was Mephibosheth.
>
> —2 SAMUEL 4:4

Mephibosheth was dropped when he was in the arms of someone he trusted, and the incident left him lame, handicapped, and crippled. I don't know who dropped you and made you crippled. I don't know if it was your mother, your father, your first husband, your babysitter, the government, or your boss. But if you are crippled in your emotions or your spirit, it probably happened because someone didn't care for you or love you the way he or she should have.

After Mephibosheth was dropped, he was sent to live in a place called Lodebar. *Lodebar* means "without pasture." It's a desert, a wilderness, a place of shame, a city of despair.

I don't know who made you live in the wilderness, in a place of shame, but I do know this—it's not God's intention for you to stay there.

Then king David sent, and fetched him out of the
house of Machir, the son of Ammiel, from Lodebar.
—2 SAMUEL 9:5

David said, "Go get him!" David didn't ask if Mephibosheth
felt like coming. He didn't accept *no* for an answer. He simply
said, "Go get him by the hand and bring him to me. I made a
covenant, and he is the recipient of that covenant I made."

When Mephibosheth came into the presence of David, he
made a pitiful statement: "What is thy servant, that thou
shouldest look upon such a dead
dog as I am?" (2 Sam. 9:8). Have you
ever felt like Mephibosheth? Many
of us have that "dead-dog" syn-
drome. We do not see ourselves as
God sees us, nor do we see God as
He really is. Our perception has been
distorted because somewhere in life,
somebody we trusted dropped us.

God is not on the judgment seat. Our heavenly Father is in the family den, ready to open His arms and receive us as His beloved children.

Like poor Mephibosheth, we see
ourselves as worthless dogs, impossible to love, and unworthy of God's
favor. How could I crawl up in the
lap of a heavenly Father and call Him "Daddy"? He would eventually see the ugly, unlovable side of me and therefore abandon
me.

Like our views of ourselves, our concepts of who God is and of
His character are often formed through sick, twisted ways of
thinking. These are based on encounters and experiences we have
with the people who have wounded us along the way. If we don't
understand the character and nature of God, then we will never

really be able to receive the person of God or any of the gifts or benefits He has for us.

What about you? Do you have a false concept of yourself or of God because of warped thinking?

Grapes or Giants?

There is a vivid account of this truth found in Numbers, chapter 13. The children of Israel have left Egypt after hundreds of years in bondage as slaves. God has delivered them from the hands of the Egyptians and is leading them into the Promised Land of Canaan. Between the "bondage land" and the "Promised Land" stood the wilderness.

If you are in a wilderness place right now, let me encourage you. God's Word reminds us, "And let us not be weary in well doing: for in due season we shall reap, if we faint not" (Gal. 6:9). *You will come out of your wilderness!* Keep in mind that there is a purpose for this season of your journey. Although many times it is difficult to see or to understand, God is diligently working on your behalf. He is with you in your wilderness. And, like the children of Israel, you will be able to endure all the obstacles in the wilderness because you can be assured that you will eventually come to the Land of Promise.

When the Israelites got near the "place of blessing," Moses, their leader, sent one man from each tribe to go spy out the land and to bring back a report of what he had observed. (See Numbers 13:17–20.) It was critical that they gain a vision of the land into which God wanted to lead them. If you don't have a vision of where you are going, how will you know when you get there?

Twelve men were selected. They went into the land during the harvest season, and there were grapes everywhere. The Israelites had been in the wilderness for years, and they had not seen fruit like that for a very long time. Now every time they turned to the right, they saw grapes, or to the left, they saw more grapes. Everywhere they looked they saw luscious clusters of grapes.

Grapes are symbolic of God's blessings. And what a blessing this was—it was such an awesome experience to reach out and pick clusters of grapes, pomegranates, and figs and to carry them back to the people on the other side of the Promised Land (Num. 13:23). It would give them a foretaste of what God was going to do.

When the spies returned after forty days of searching out the land, they went before their leaders, Moses and Aaron, and all the people of Israel with this report:

> And they told him, and said, We came unto the land whither thou sentest us, and surely it floweth with milk and honey; and this is the fruit of it. Nevertheless the people be strong that dwell in the land, and the cities are walled, and very great: and moreover we saw the children of Anak there. The Amalekites dwell in the land of the south: and the Hittites, and the Jebusites, and the Amorites, dwell in the mountains: and the Canaanites dwell by the sea, and by the coast of Jordan.
>
> And Caleb stilled the people before Moses, and said, Let us go up at once, and possess it; for we are well able to overcome it. But the men that went up with him said, We be not able to go up against the people; for they are stronger than we. And they brought up an evil report of the land which they had searched unto the children of Israel, saying, The land, through which we have gone to search it, is a land that eateth up the inhabitants thereof; and all the people that we saw in it are men of a great stature. And there we saw the giants, the sons of Anak, which come of the giants: and we

were in our own sight as grasshoppers, and so we were
in their sight.

—NUMBERS 13:27–33

Twelve men were exposed to the same thing—but they did not
come back with the same report. How can twelve people see the
same thing but have an entirely different perspective? Because of
differences in perception. This is crucial, because your perception
will determine your actions.

Promises and Problems

When the spies made their way across the Jordan River, they saw
a land that flowed with milk and honey and flourished with
crops and fruit. They saw the prosperity and the provision of
God. But as with anything in life,
they also saw the problems
standing in the way of the promise.
Now, as then, we cannot get the
promises without dealing with the
problems.

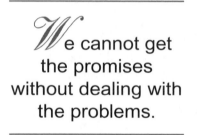

We cannot get
the promises
without dealing with
the problems.

You've probably heard the
saying, "Anything worth having is
worth fighting for." More often
than not, a battle precedes a blessing. In the case of the Israelites,
God showed them the promise, but He also showed them the
problems that stood in their way.

The number one problem for the children of Israel was a
group of men known as "the sons of Anak." These people pos-
sessed the land that God had promised to His people. And the
sons of Anak were a big problem in more ways than one. They
stood somewhere between nine and eleven feet tall! You may not

remember these people by name, but surely you recall a descendent of theirs named Goliath. These warriors had a tendency to be dressed in brass, bearing shields, swords, and all kinds of deadly weapons. The children of Israel were just common shepherds. They did not know anything about fighting at this point. They simply wanted to possess the promises, but all the problems loomed ominously in their way.

Many of us have been waiting for the giants to get out of our own Promised Land, but they aren't going anywhere. We've sat back and waited until everything was nice and easy, then we could move forward and possess our promise. That is not how it works. The people who get the victory are the people who look at the grapes (the blessings), then look at the giants (the problems), and determine, "I want the grapes badly enough that if I have to fight these giants to get them, then so be it."

If you are going to inherit what God has for you, then you must become obsessed with the grapes. What you look at longest will become strongest in your life! So focus your eyes on the "grapes"—the wonderful promises of God. We cannot look at the grapes, then look at the giants, then back at the grapes, and back at the giants. This will cause confusion and eventually make us unstable. "A double minded man is unstable in all of his ways" (James 1:8).

Although twelve men went over into the Promised Land and saw the same thing, they did not see it in the same way. In fact, the Bible records that most of them became so frightened by the giants that they forgot about the grapes. Ten of them talked about how big the giants were, how tough the situation was, and how impossible the battle was going to be. They based their reports and their conclusions upon what they perceived. They perceived themselves as small as grasshoppers, and they were quite sure the Anakites thought the Israelites were small as grasshoppers, too. People see us the way we see ourselves. That is why, unconsciously, we attract what we think we deserve.

The Bible says a whole generation died in the wilderness simply because they did not have the right attitude. Our attitude will determine our perception, and perception is everything. The problem that you are facing right now is really not what matters. What matters is how you perceive the problem. If you cannot change your perception, it is possible that you may die in the wilderness. If you can change the way you perceive a situation, a circumstance, or a relationship, then you can come out of the wilderness and enter into the promise. But to move into the promises of God, you have to learn to trust God. The real issue is whether you believe that God will fight for you in the battle and whether you know He loves you enough to give you the desires of your heart.

Learning to Trust

In my years as a new believer, I wanted to trust, to confide in someone without fear. But how could I trust? Even more difficult, *whom* could I trust? The Bible offers a solution to this question:

> Trust in the LORD with all thine heart; and lean not unto thine own understanding. In all thy ways acknowledge him, and he shall direct thy paths.
> —PROVERBS 3:5–6

Initially, the starting point to reestablishing trust is to put your confidence in the Lord. The writer of Proverbs says to trust God in every area. Don't even trust yourself; in everything, trust only God. This was very difficult for me to learn to do. Other people had hurt me, had done me wrong—how could I know that God would not hurt me? This is where I had everything topsy-turvy and upside down. I looked at God through eyesight damaged by people to whom I had looked with trust. I saw God through people instead of seeing people through God.

Whatever "lens" you are looking through will establish your focus on the object to which you are looking. I was looking through the wrong lens. I was afraid to trust God. Of course He never did anything to instigate this mistrust, but nevertheless, it was still there. It took me a long time, but eventually I got it through my head that God is faithful. He is consistent and has my best interests at heart. He would never disappoint me or let me down. Over time, my relationship with Him developed enough so that I could not only trust Him, but He could also trust me.

I can only trust people when I have first trusted God. Let me explain. We read in John 2:24–25:

> But Jesus did not commit himself unto them, because he knew all men, and needed not that any should tes- tify of man: for he knew what was in man.

The word *commit* means "to trust." In this passage we see that Jesus did not trust Himself to man because He knew what people were made of. People *will* disappoint you. They *will* let you down. That is why Proverbs 3 says that you should not even trust yourself (Prov. 3:7). Your flesh is weak; it will lead you astray. You cannot trust your flesh in a compromising situation—it will fail you. Jesus was saying that He knows people are fallible, but God is infallible. It is dangerous to commit or trust yourself into the hands of someone when you have not first trusted in God. You inevitably will get hurt, simply because man is weak and, without

God, wicked. Only when I develop a trust relationship with God can I discern with whom to develop a trust relationship here on earth. I must commit myself to God in order to develop trust relationships with people.

It is necessary to your well-being and spiritual and emotional development to have people in your life whom you can trust. I believe that Paul clued us in on the key to qualifying people for relationships built on trust, when he advised people to follow him as he followed Christ. (See 1 Corinthians 4:15–16; 11:1.)

When I began to study the Word of God, I discovered that God works through spiritual authority and protocol. Many of my blessings will be released through the person or people whom God has placed in my life as spiritual authorities. If I cannot trust them, then I miss out on much of what God has for me. God does not work through renegades. He is serious about His system of protocol. I can trust people *if* they are trusting God.

Randy has been greatly used by God in my life to bring healing and restoration. God will use people in your life for healing and blessing, just as the enemy used people for his purpose of destruction. If you refuse to receive the person because you cannot trust him or her, then you miss out on God's blessing for your life. When Randy and I became serious in our relationship, I was still shaky about trusting a person. I developed a self-defensive attitude toward him. I had unconsciously determined to push him out before he had opportunity to leave me.

One day in an emotional upheaval I cried out to the Lord, and God spoke to my spirit, saying, "Randy was Mine before he was yours." A sudden peace calmed all of my fears when I realized that Randy had first committed himself to God. If there was some unknown thing in his life that could hurt me, God would deal with him. Suddenly I understood that trust can be developed and nurtured in a relationship as two people submit themselves first to God.

There are too many children of God living with paranoid feelings because someone has hurt them. Yes, people will disappoint you, but think about all the people you have disappointed. At some point you must work through your barriers and build healthy relationships. This can only be accomplished when your confidence is in the Lord.

Psalm 62:8 advises, "Trust in him at all times; ye people, pour out your heart before him: God is a refuge for us." You will not be disappointed when you trust in the Lord. Trust is a product of love. God wants you to know that He loves you, and once you know that, you will finally be able to trust Him.

God Is a Promise Keeper

God is faithful. He is not like the people you meet every day who talk big but have small memories. If God has promised you something, you can be sure you will have it. You can learn this lesson from God's dealings with David.

God told the prophet Samuel to go down to Jesse's house and anoint one of his boys to be king (1 Sam. 16:1). When Samuel got there, he met each family member and eventually asked, "Is there another boy?" It does not matter how many people have looked you over, have sidestepped you, or have counted you unworthy; when God promotes you, the hand of man cannot stop Him.

"Yes, there is one more boy, but he's out tending to the sheep."

I can hear them saying, "Are you sure he's the one? He is always out there singing and writing love letters to God. He is a little strange—dancing, twirling, and blowing kisses to God. He writes poetry and plays his harp for the Lord."

Samuel nodded his head and responded, "Go and get him!"

After one look at this young shepherd boy, Samuel anointed David to be king over Israel. And he was to be the greatest king Israel would ever know until Jesus Himself reigns as King of kings over all the earth.

But David didn't become the king the minute Samuel anointed him. While Saul was sitting on the throne, David was anointed for the throne. That is why you should not worry when you see someone else in the position God has promised you. What should you do in the meantime?

> *If God has promised you something, it will come to pass. There might be a waiting period, but it will come to pass!*

> Humble yourselves therefore under the mighty hand of God, that he may exalt you in due time.
> —1 PETER 5:6

God is faithful to fulfill every promise He gives to us. Hebrews 6:12 explains that the promises of God are inherited through faith and patience. If God has promised you something, it will come to pass. There might be a waiting period, but it *will* come to pass! I believe many of us throw in the towel and quit just before we break through to the promise God has for us.

It is so vital to understand that the promises of God have to come true, because "God is not a man, that he should lie; neither the son of man, that he should repent: hath he said, and shall he not do it? Or hath he spoken, and shall he not make it good?"

(Num. 23:19). Add that statement to the fact that He loves you, and you will begin to see who God isn't—He isn't like anyone you've ever known before.

Personal Reflections

Think About This

Read the quotes from this chapter below. After each one take a moment to reflect on how the statement links to a feeling or experience in your own life. Give your own personal reaction to each statement.

1. If we don't understand the character and nature of God, then we will never really be able to receive the person of God or any of the gifts or benefits He has for us. Take a few minutes to think about God's character and then list at least six positive characteristics about Him. Beside each characteristic, explain how that characteristic has touched your life.

_____

_____

_____

_____

_____

_____

2. If you can change the way you perceive a situation, a circumstance, or a relationship, then you can come out of the wilderness and enter into the promise. But to move into the promises of God, you have to learn to trust God. The real issue is whether you believe that God will fight for you in the battle and whether you know He loves you enough to give you the desires of

your heart. Tell about one situation where because you trusted God with the circumstances, He was able to lead you out of that wilderness experience and into a blessing from Him.

---

3. It is necessary to your well-being and spiritual and emotional development to have people in your life whom you can trust. I believe that Paul clued us in on the key to qualifying people for relationships built on trust when he advised people to follow him as he followed Christ. (See 1 Corinthians 4:15–16; 11:1.) Describe a time in your own life when a trusted friend or advisor helped you understand a situation you were facing.

Talk to God

> *Father, destroy in my mind and heart every image of You that does not represent who You really are. Change every false perception of You that blocks me from knowing and loving You the way I should. Don't allow my hurtful relationships with people— all those things that have created mistrust—to keep me from trusting You. In every area where I have been hardened, please soften my heart, making it pliable and tender toward You. Lord, make me the trustworthy person that You have called me to be. Amen.*

FIVE

Forgiving the Unforgivable

After dating for a while, Randy and I became pretty serious about each other; before long he began to talk about marriage. I so desperately needed and wanted the relationship with him. I really believed that Randy was the partner God had planned for my life. But all my insecurities and fears made me suspicious and cynical. I didn't really think we could ever achieve a stable relationship.

One day we were at a park, and Randy was pushing me on the swing. He gave me a big shove from behind, then he scurried around in front of me. He pointed his finger at me and announced, "You will be my wife!"

I jumped off the swing and stared directly into his face, absolutely traumatized by his words. He smiled at me ever so gently and whispered that God had told him that I would, indeed, be his wife.

Following that occasion, what should have been a wonderful time of my life turned sour. Randy was so confident, so sure. He knew that he had heard from God, and that was how it was going to be. I, on the other hand, was overwhelmed by fear and doubt. I freaked out. I still assumed that everyone in my life would eventually reject me and abandon me. In fact, I could not imagine it any other way. So, in keeping with my old ways of thinking, I decided to do the rejecting myself.

For no logical reason, I began to call an old boyfriend. I didn't go out with him, and I didn't involve myself in any unholy way. But I was compromising the beautiful relationship gift God had given me, and I knew it. It was illogical that I would do something so foolish, yet what did logic have to do with it? I was scared and obviously was not thinking clearly. I was allowing myself to be led by my emotions, fears, and insecurities.

As time went by, I became more and more tormented, knowing that I must be honest with Randy regarding my contact with this other person. I finally did what I should have done all along. I began to count the cost.

Of course, I assumed this would be the end of the relationship. Randy had always made it clear that anything could be worked through as long as there was honesty and integrity between us. I had violated both. How could I have been so stupid? What had I done? I loved this man. My heart was broken, but I knew that I deserved what was coming to me. I had brought this on myself and deserved the consequences of my actions. I was sure that this would be the termination of the relationship.

I took Randy out to his favorite restaurant. I made sure he sat on the inside of the booth so he could not escape. It was a public place, too, so I assumed that he could not make too much of a scene. I had planned the evening methodically, foreseeing every move and outcome.

Halfway into the evening Randy knew something was bothering me. "What's wrong?" he asked.

I proceeded to tell him. He laid down his fork and stared into the distance. He said, "Paula, please excuse me." His face looked as if someone had just knocked the breath out of him. Why was he not yelling at me and telling me how horrible I was? The expression on his face was not one of anger but of hurt. He excused himself and walked outside.

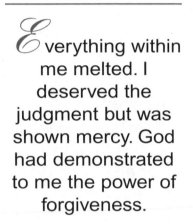

*E*verything within me melted. I deserved the judgment but was shown mercy. God had demonstrated to me the power of forgiveness.

This was not the reaction I had expected, because in all of my planning I had failed to plan on the power of God in a man who has been forgiven. Jesus once explained that those who have been forgiven a great deal are capable of loving deeply. He told his companions, "Wherefore I say unto thee, Her sins, which are many, are forgiven; for she loved much: but to whom little is forgiven, the same loveth little" (Luke 7:47).

I sat alone in that restaurant for what seemed like an eternity, feeling completely unsure of what to expect next. Randy walked back in after about an hour. He looked me in my eyes and simply said, "We will work through this. I love you."

Everything within me melted. I deserved judgment but was shown mercy. God had demonstrated to me the power of forgiveness. Receiving forgiveness from Randy was important, and when I did, I learned a lot about unconditional love. But God wasn't finished with me yet.

A Little Girl and a Time Machine

Randy and I began working together in ministry. Our wonderful pastor, Dr. T. L. Lowery, allowed us to fulfill our life's call and commission in both restoration and evangelism. As a couple, we headed up the church's bus ministry and evangelism outreach. I taught the Word of God to the children and to some of their mothers.

If I wanted forgiveness from my heavenly Father, I had to forgive those who had abused me. . . . There were no negotiations and no compromises, just one simple command—forgive!

One morning a little girl about five years old ran up to me, and for some reason she began talking to me. Before I knew it, she was sharing with me a horrifying tale of abuse. I had no doubt about the truthfulness of her story. The neglect was obvious: Her hair was matted and dirty, and her dress was tattered and torn. Worst of all, when I looked into her eyes it seemed as if I were staring into a deep, dark tunnel that led nowhere. I knew that look all too well.

All at once it seemed as if I had somehow found my way into a time machine and was staring at myself. I located a co-worker and asked her to minister to the little girl. I told her to get every bit of help we could possibly provide for this little girl. Then I literally ran out of the room.

In the days that followed, I was consumed with roller-coaster emotions. Just when I seemed to have moved forward twenty feet, I was knocked back forty. I couldn't find my balance. I wrestled with old feelings and thoughts, with ugly memories, and long-forgotten faces. This situation was doubly painful for me. On the one hand, I was beating myself up, thinking how selfish I had been to think about my past when the little girl was being abused in the present. On the other hand, the incident had triggered a devastating response in me.

Once again, I was raging at my own abusers. I had thought they were long gone, but now they were with me again. They were reappearing in my dreams. They were riding in the car with me, and I was not charging them cab fare. They were eating dinner with me and not paying for their meals. They were living in an apartment, rent free, somewhere inside my head. They had me at their mercy, and once again I was their victim.

I went into my living room, stretched myself across the floor, and began to weep. The pain was immense, and I was tired of hurting. Would I ever get beyond this? Jesus' words gently played and replayed in my soul:

> For if ye forgive men their trespasses, your heavenly Father will also forgive you: But if ye forgive not men their trespasses, neither will your Father forgive your trespasses.
>
> —MATTHEW 6:14–15

In that dark hour, it seemed so unfair, so impossible. If I wanted forgiveness from my heavenly Father, I had to forgive those who had abused me. There were no ifs, ands, or buts about it. There were no negotiations and no compromises, just one simple command—*forgive!*

Father Knows Best

I have a wonderful son whose name is Brad. On many occasions, especially when he was very young, I would tell Brad to do something simply because I said so. As his parent, I had an advantaged point of insight; I could see some things that he could not yet discern. When he tried to argue, I didn't reason with him on any issue that I knew involved his well-being or safety. I always made my instructions matter-of-fact, saying, "This is how it is going to be!" I know that one day he will understand how and why his best interests were kept in mind, even though he didn't (maybe he still doesn't) always agree with me. But as his parent, I can see things that he can't.

Just as Brad can't always see that my demands on certain issues are for his best interests, neither could I see at the time that my heavenly Father had my best interests in mind. I did not understand that forgiveness was much more for my benefit than for the benefit of my transgressors.

In Matthew 18:21–22 we read:

> Then came Peter to him, and said, Lord, how oft shall my brother sin against me, and I forgive him? till seven times? Jesus saith unto him, I say not unto thee, Until seven times: but, Until seventy times seven.

Jesus' message to Peter couldn't have been clearer. Forgive and keep on forgiving! Walk in a continual state of forgiveness! No matter how many times you have been hurt, wounded, or abused, forgive your transgressor. No matter how hideous the offenses have been, forgive the offender.

"Lord, I Can't . . . "

Sometimes we fool ourselves. For years I went through a "confession" routine of forgiveness. Repeatedly, I said that I had forgiven the people who had violated me, victimized me, and so deeply hurt me. Over and over I declared that I had forgiven them. Yet years had passed, and still I was occupied with the thoughts of my offenders. Some of them I would never see again. You have heard the saying "out of sight, out of mind." Not so with the people who had hurt me. Some of them were dead, but they were still very much alive to me. Others I had to see on occasion, and I always dreaded it. When these unavoidable encounters occurred, I thought, *I may be in the same room, but do not make me look you in the face or have to speak to you!*

I was a prisoner, imprisoned by my own hurts and bitterness. I was trapped by memories of past pain. How could the people who had injured me be so free and so happy? It made me angry, and my anger—perhaps it was even envy—was rooted in the fact that others had found a kind of freedom that I had not yet experienced.

Trying to sort out all the confusion in my heart, I began to cry out to God. "Lord, I can't get over this on my own. The hurt is way too deep, and it's eating me up!" Once I said those words, within a split second, a sudden peace came over me. I knew it was the presence of God. It seemed as if a still, small voice inside of me responded and declared, "Allow Me the ability to place forgiveness in you."

What? That was a strange idea. But it gradually dawned on me that I had been trying to forgive my transgressors with my own will and determination, and I was simply incapable of such a huge task. I could not forgive in my own strength. However, I did have the ability to allow the Holy Spirit to forgive *through* me. I yielded myself to the Spirit of God. I told God that He had my permission to place forgiveness within my heart.

The lesson was clear—forgiveness is a choice. We have the choice to hold resentment and bitterness inside forever. Or we have the choice to yield ourselves to the Spirit of God and to allow Him to place His forgiveness within us. I did the latter, and within moments I was free. I was free from my captors who had held me hostage for years.

To my amazement, for the first time in my life I actually felt compassion toward the people who had abused and molested me. It is difficult to explain, but where previously there was anger, hatred, hurt, and confusion, I now felt mercy.

It was as if a veil had been lifted off, and I saw things the way they really were. I understood that most of them had acted out what had been done to them. I understood that they had abused because they had been abused. They had rejected because they had been rejected. I even understood something beyond that:

> For we wrestle not against flesh and blood, but against principalities, against powers, against the rulers of the darkness of this world, against spiritual wickedness in high places.
>
> —EPHESIANS 6:12

I finally was able to see that my enemy was not the person who had transgressed me; my enemy was the evil spirit that had influenced that person.

Perhaps you are saying, "Paula, you don't understand. I cannot forgive! What happened is unforgivable!" I really do understand your feelings. But you are essentially saying that God is not big enough. You are declaring that the work completed at Calvary was not good enough. You *can* forgive, although the ability to do so is not contained within yourself. Only through the work of the Holy Spirit can you obtain the ability to forgive every person who ever wronged you, and to forgive every act that ever wounded you.

Matthew records a powerful parable about forgiveness and an unmerciful servant.

> Then his lord, after that he had called him, said unto him, O thou wicked servant, I forgave thee all that debt, because thou desiredst me: Shouldest not thou also have had compassion on thy fellowservant, even as I had pity on thee? And his lord was wroth, and delivered him to the tormentors, till he should pay all that was due unto him. So likewise shall my heavenly Father do also unto you, if ye *from your hearts* forgive not every one his brother their trespasses.
> —MATTHEW 18:32–35, ITALICS ADDED

The Scriptures couldn't be more clear—we must forgive *from our hearts*. I had been making a daily confession of forgiveness, but it had not emanated from my heart. It had become a verbal routine, a superficial gesture. That is why I had not truly experienced the fruit of forgiveness. Only God can do a heart work. Only the Spirit of God can change the heart of a man or woman. Until I involved God in the forgiveness process, I could not experience the freedom that is found in true forgiveness.

Forgiven and Forgiving

Yes, there is freedom in forgiveness. I believe this is so beautifully illustrated in Psalm 32, which is a psalm of instruction. It refers to the time in David's life that we read about in 2 Samuel 11 and 12. David had committed adultery with Bathsheba, and then he had tried to cover up his sins. For one year David suffered over his transgression. As he wrote, he expressed his anguish, his grief, and the suffering he had experienced. He also expressed for us the power of forgiveness and deliverance.

> Blessed is he whose transgression is forgiven, whose sin is covered. Blessed is the man unto whom the LORD imputeth not iniquity, and in whose spirit there is no guile. When I kept silence, my bones waxed old through my roaring all the day long.
> For day and night thy hand was heavy upon me: my moisture is turned into the drought of summer. Selah. I acknowledged my sin unto thee, and mine iniquity have I not hid. I said, I will confess my transgressions unto the LORD; and thou forgavest the iniquity of my sin. Selah.
>
> —PSALM 32:1–5

David says, "Blessed," or happy, ecstatic, exuberant, and thrilled, is the man whose transgression is forgiven. A *transgression* is an offense. It means we have gone too far and crossed the line. Many of us know what it is to go "too far." David understood what it meant to offend God, to offend man, and even to offend himself. He shares with us that the key to freedom and happiness is found in forgiveness. The word *forgiven* means "to be loosed from." He says, "I am happy when I have been loosed from my offense."

In verse 2, David goes on to express: "Blessed [happy] is the man unto whom the LORD imputeth not iniquity." To *impute* means "to be reckoned or put to the account of someone; to charge with." Happy is the person whom the Lord does not charge with sin! When we saints get to heaven, we are not going to be like the sinners. We will not be charged with sin, because we have been loosed through the completed work at Calvary.

David then reveals to us that when he tried to cover up his sin, keeping his silence, that buried sin did something bad to him. He said that his bones waxed old. When we hold unforgiveness and sin inside us, it will affect our physical bodies. David tossed and turned all night until he acknowledged his sin! The moment he acknowledged it and confessed it, simultaneously God forgave it. There is freedom in forgiveness. There is freedom from guilt when we receive forgiveness. There is freedom from bitterness when we forgive others.

> Keep thy heart with all diligence; for out of it are the issues of life.
>
> —PROVERBS 4:23

The word *keep* is equivalent to "guard." As an officer would watch over a prison and protect it against intruders and escapees, so are we to guard our hearts. Whatever is allowed to get inside us will eventually flow out of us. That is why we must come to the conclusion that no person, no act, no offense, no hurt, and no bitter memory is worth the toxic effect it has on our hearts.

If we do not guard our hearts, unforgiveness can become a stumbling block, blinding us to the will of God.

> He that saith he is in the light, and hateth his brother, is in darkness even until now. He that loveth his brother abideth in the light, and there is none occasion of stumbling in him. But he that hateth his brother is in darkness, and walketh in darkness, and knoweth not whither he goeth, because that darkness hath blinded his eyes.
>
> —1 JOHN 2:9–11

As God's children, we desperately need to know the will of God. All of the promises that He has for us are found within His will for our lives. When we choose to walk in unforgiveness, we become blinded. We are unable to see or discern the will of God for us. God has so many wonderful blessings for His children, and it is His desire for us to be blessed and to prosper. "Beloved, I wish above all things that thou mayest prosper and be in health, even as thy soul prospereth" (3 John 2). The Lord wants you to know the clear path of His will, but unforgiveness will cloud your way.

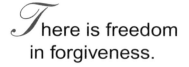

There is freedom in forgiveness.

It is obvious that God demands forgiveness for our benefit. We can be free from our transgressors by allowing God to do what only He can do—forgive the unforgivable. And, in response, we can forgive those who have trespassed against us. Grace and forgiveness are synonymous with each other. They go together hand in hand.

The best definition for *grace* is "unmerited favor." Grace is undeserved. We cannot work for it or earn it. Long before I allowed God to forgive through me, I read the many accounts of forgiveness recorded in the Bible over and over. I knew very well that God in His grace and mercy forgave people continually. It did not seem to matter how heinous the offense, God always forgave. This seemed right to me—after all, He is God. For many years, I lived with a double standard. It was great to receive forgiveness, but I refused to give it! Instead, I continued to harbor resentment toward people who had treated me unjustly.

Forgiveness isn't just hard. In human terms, it can be impossible. But we know, "If thou canst believe, all things are possible to him that believeth" (Mark 9:23). By recognizing our need to forgive, we take the first step. By realizing that we do not have the ability to forgive in our own strength, we take the second step. By asking God to come in and forgive through us, we are cleansed of the bitter poison in our soul, and we take the final step back onto the bright and blessed pathway of His perfect will.

Personal Reflections

Think About This

Read the quotes from this chapter below. After each one take a moment to reflect on how the statement links to a feeling or experience in your own life. Give your own personal reaction to each statement.

1. In that dark hour, it seemed so unfair, so impossible. If I wanted forgiveness from my heavenly Father, I had to forgive those who had abused me. There were no ifs, ands, or buts about it. There were no negotiations and no compromises, just one simple command—*forgive!* The author has just described the moment when she realized her need to forgive others. Describe a moment like that in your experience.

2. David tossed and turned all night until he acknowledged his sin! The moment he acknowledged it and confessed it, simultaneously God forgave it. There is freedom in forgiveness. There is freedom from guilt when we receive forgiveness. There is freedom from bitterness when we forgive others. Think about that moment you just described in number 1 above. Now

describe how you felt after you stepped out in an act of forgiveness for someone who had wronged you.

_____

_____

_____

3. As God's children, we desperately need to know the will of God. When we choose to walk in unforgiveness, we become blinded. The Lord wants you to know the clear path of His will, but unforgiveness will cloud your way. Is there a place where you have been seeking to know the will of God? Is there a chance that unforgiveness in that situation has blinded the knowledge of His will? Are you ready to offer forgiveness regarding the situation? How can you do this?

_____

_____

_____

Talk to God

> *Lord, please give me the ability to forgive where I have been unable or unwilling to do so before. I have good intentions, but unless You forgive others through me, I cannot forgive at all. Reveal to me areas of bitterness and grudges that I may not recognize, and cleanse me of all resentment. If I have offended or if I hold offenses, release me and my transgressor through the power of Jesus' shed blood. Create in me a clean heart, O Lord, and renew a right spirit within me. Amen.*

Six

Broken Promises, Shattered Dreams

On a beautiful sunny afternoon I visited my grand-parents in their small country town. I was seven years old, and my granddaddy took me by the hand and walked with me to the five-and-dime store. Once I got inside, I ran straight for the toy section. My grandfather quickly followed behind me, smiling at my very obvious excitement over all the different toys.

"Look, Granddaddy!" I exclaimed as I picked up a baby doll. "Oh, how beautiful!"

He carefully observed my every move, obviously delighted to see me so happy. Then I saw it! The biggest, prettiest baby doll I had ever laid my eyes on. She stood about three feet tall, wore a pink lace dress, and her long blonde locks were arrayed with ribbons. I stood speech-less, my mouth open in amazement. I pointed to her, my little heart thumping with great hope and the longing to have her all to myself.

"Do you like her?" my granddaddy asked.

Did I like her? I loved her!

"One of these days I'll buy her for you, Paula," he said with a big smile.

Great joy swept over me, knowing that someday she would be mine. Christmas was just around the corner. Surely Christmas was in the back of Grandaddy's mind, and that would be when he'd give me the beautiful doll.

Christmas came and went, but no baby doll.

Maybe she'll be here on my birthday, I reasoned. My birthday came and went, but no baby doll. Many years passed, and still no doll. On every occasion that presented an opportunity for gift giving, I looked for that beautiful doll. Unbelievably, even at eighteen years of age I was still looking for her. She never arrived. Even though I received other beautiful gifts, there was no big, pink baby doll.

That doll was just one of the many broken promises that I experienced in my young life. It seems so insignificant now—just another plaything. But looking back, I can see that it wasn't so much the gift I desired as it was my yearning for someone to be faithful and to keep a promise made to me. To me the doll would have meant that someone cared, that someone thought I was special, and that somebody loved me. The unfulfilled promise reaffirmed that there was something in me that was unlovable.

A Broken World

Growing up as a young girl, there were times when I felt as if life had popped my bubble. My hopes and dreams were shattered many times. Life presented me with more than my share of disappointments, many tears, and many setbacks. I could not understand why it was *my* daddy who had to die—he had convinced me that he would always be my Superman. I couldn't see why terrible, cruel things happened to me and why the promise of a "good life" never seemed to be fulfilled.

When promises are not kept and dreams are shattered, people's hearts are broken. This is my definition of a "broken world."

Whether your heart was broken as the result of someone else's sinful or treacherous behavior or whether it was broken by a self-inflicted blow doesn't matter. Too many broken hearts create a broken world, no matter how the damage was done in the first place.

I wish I could tell you that brokenness is avoidable, that it is escapable. However, tears are an unavoidable aspect of our earthly existence. They are a part of everyone's experience. Joy and sorrow are intermingled together day and night to produce the interplay of light and darkness we call life. I have discovered something about pain. It is not prejudiced. Pain does not care if you are young or old, rich or poor, black or white, smart or ignorant. Pain is an equal-opportunity experience.

Trouble has no prerequisites. Sooner or later it knocks on your door. And when it knocks, you come to understand that there is a vast difference between a national dilemma and a personal dilemma. We are moved with compassion when we see starving children in various nations on television, but that feeling of compassion pales in comparison to the agony we feel when we cannot feed our own babies. A personal crisis can shatter your world.

Many of the great disappointments that we experience in life result from our great expectations. We expect things to go a certain way, and when they don't, we are disappointed. When we are disappointed, we easily become disillusioned. When we are disillusioned, we are unable to make wise decisions.

I expected that baby doll. When it never came, I was disappointed, which in turn eventually caused me to come to the conclusion that I was unlovable. Nothing could have been more further from the truth, but I based my conclusion on my unmet expectation, and I acted upon it. In my lifetime, I have made many wrong decisions because of unfulfilled expectations, which eventually led me to become cynical, deciding that it would be easier not to expect anything from anyone than to carry around a load of hurt and disappointment.

> *Y*ou were created with a purpose and a destiny. God's best work still lies ahead for you.

Many times in my life things have not turned out the way I had hoped or planned. Early in adulthood, I found myself wondering, *How can God get glory out of this mess?* Perhaps you have asked the same question. Maybe your dream wasn't shattered by the loss of your father, as mine was. Maybe it was a different man—one who told you that he would love you until "death do you part," yet he walked out on you. Maybe it was a relative or friend who violated your trust and left you broken. Maybe your disappointment came through death or disease or divorce.

If God can take a little messed-up Mississippi girl, turn my pain into power, and use me for His glory, then He can do it for you! Like me, you were created with a purpose and a destiny. God's best work still lies ahead for you. Do not allow your circumstances—past or present—to get the best of you. Allow God to take what the enemy meant for your harm, and use it for His good and glory.

God's Best Work

I recall lying on my bed one night when I was around twenty years of age, staring at the ceiling for what seemed to be hours. I replayed the events in my life like a movie in slow motion. I went over each event meticulously, asking the kinds of endless questions that lead nowhere. Suddenly I burst out crying. I grabbed my pillow and pulled it to my chest. I cried with such intensity that it felt as if my lungs would explode.

The onset of my outburst came when I realized that I was not a whole or healthy person, that I had made choices that could not be reversed, and now they had produced a "harvest" in my life. As a little girl I had dreamed of being a wife and a mother, of having a family. I was now lying on my bed after going through a divorce, full of insecurities and the fear of rejection and abandonment. I was asking myself, *Who would ever want me now after this mess?* My world was broken.

God does His finest work in the lives of broken people.

> The LORD is nigh unto them that are of a broken heart;
> and saveth such as be of a contrite spirit.
> —PSALM 34:18

Pain can become a conduit for power. I eventually discovered that what was meant to destroy us can actually be what makes us strong and whole. What was supposed to be a stumbling block in our lives can actually become a stepping stone.

I have learned to deeply appreciate the scripture found in Romans 8:28:

> And we know that all things work together for good to
> them that love God, to them who are the called
> according to his purpose.

It might not seem as though any good could possibly come out
of your situation. How can God take your mess and get any glory?
But interestingly, transforming messes is actually what He does
best. I have found that God communes with, blesses, and uses
people not because they are perfect in life, but because they have
painfully discovered the way of grace.

God does His most powerful work when we are weak, empty,
and helpless. That is not the state we like to be in, but it is the
condition out of which God builds masterpieces. We like *full*.
God likes *empty*. In fact, emptiness is a necessary first step to
being filled. You can see that in the Book of Genesis. In Genesis
1:1, God created the heaven and earth. But between verses 1 and
2, there was a problem that provoked God—the earth was
without form. It was empty and void. The Bible records that the
Spirit of God moved and began to solve the problem.

Is your life broken and empty right now? It is not the end for
you, but merely an opportunity for God to move, to bring order,
to do a miraculous, creative work. In 2 Corinthians 12:9, Jesus
told His faithful apostle Paul, "My grace is sufficient for thee: for
my strength is made perfect in weakness." When you have
nothing to offer God but your weakness and your broken heart,
give it to Him anyway. He can turn your ashes into beauty.

Beauty for Ashes

This principle is so beautifully illustrated in the life of King David
as found in 1 Chronicles, chapter 21. David has sinned. He has
taken a census of Israel—against the instruction of God. There are

consequences for sin. The Lord offers David a choice of three different punishments: three years of famine, three months under the sword of his enemies, or three days under the judgment of God.

David had an intimate relationship with God; he knew God's character well. David reasoned, *I'm in a hard place, but I would prefer to fall into the hands of God, for great are His mercies, rather than into the hands of man.*

David chose three days of God's judgment. The Lord sent pestilence, and judgment began to fall. As an angel of the Lord was destroying Jerusalem, the Bible records that God was sorrowful for the evil and stopped the angel. In the middle of

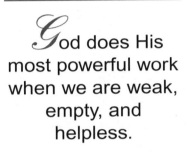

God does His most powerful work when we are weak, empty, and helpless.

judgment God gave David a word. He told him to go to the threshing floor of Ornan the Jebusite and to build Him an altar there.

What was a threshing floor? It was a place where the farm laborers beat and pounded wheat, then threw it in the air. The wind would carry away the chaff and leave the good seed to fall to the ground.

When David arrived at the threshing floor, Ornan tried to give him the oxen and instruments necessary for an offering to God. David refused to accept anything from Ornan. He would not make a sacrifice to the Lord that cost him nothing.

Instead, David built an altar, and in the middle of his brokenness, he called upon the Lord. The Lord answered David, and fire fell on the altar. David was sitting there at the threshing floor looking around—nothing was left but ashes. He had made a mess of things. His world was broken.

What can God do with ashes? What can He do with your broken world? Look what he did for David. In 2 Chronicles 3:1, we read:

> Then Solomon began to build the house of the LORD at Jerusalem in mount Moriah, where the LORD appeared unto David his father, in the place that David had prepared in the threshingfloor of Ornan the Jebusite.

When David walked away from the threshing floor, all that was left was ashes. But on those ashes, the greatest temple ever erected was built. Underneath all the splendor of the temple—the cedar, the gold, the detailed workmanship, and all the wealth—were David's ashes—ashes of disappointment and despair. David's brokenness was the foundation of Solomon's temple.

When God looks for something great to build upon, He looks for ashes. Psalm 51:17 assures us:

> The sacrifices of God are a broken spirit: a broken and a contrite heart, O God, thou wilt not despise.

God did not reject David in his brokenness. He will not reject you in yours. It is there that He can perform His finest work. When you come to God and offer Him your broken world, you will soon discover that He is the God of restoration. He is the God of renewed hope. He is the God of resurrection.

A Mother's Pain

Consider Eve, the first woman in the Bible to ever wrestle with real pain, real depression, and real brokenness. She lent her ear to the enemy, which led to the worst possible destruction—the Fall of humankind. Adam and Eve were created in the image of God, but after the Fall, every child that was conceived in the human race was born sin sick, in the likeness of Adam and Eve.

As a result of the sin that entered her life, Eve's son Cain killed her son Abel. Can you imagine the pain she must have endured? She didn't lose just one son. Abel was dead, and Cain might as well have been dead. He was there, but he was not there. He became a fugitive. What must Eve have felt? She was surely blaming herself, replaying her deception by the enemy. "What if I'd never had that conversation?" "What if I hadn't believed his lies?" "What if...?"

Eve was no doubt beating herself up for the personal failure that had caused her world to fall apart. She was thinking, *It is all over; I have made a complete mess of things.* But God wasn't finished with Eve. "And Adam knew his wife again; and she bare a son, and called his name Seth: For God, said she, hath appointed me another seed..." (Gen. 4:25). Just when you think, *It is all over—how could God ever get any glory out of this mess?*, God has a surprise for you!

Brokenness is not a permanent condition. No matter how long your world has been broken and how shattered it may be, God can pick up the pieces and create a beautiful masterpiece if you will allow Him the opportunity. What does He ask of you? If you will give Him your brokenness, your hurt, your pain, your disillusionment, your disappointments, and your fears, He can take them—the ashes of your dreams—and turn them into works of great beauty.

"Casting all your care upon him; for he careth for you" (1 Pet. 5:7). The word *casting* means to "roll over." When I examined my life as a young adult and saw nothing but brokenness, I decided to roll it over upon God. Perhaps He could reshape the marred vessel that I had become. I discovered that we serve a Lord who has been touched by the feelings of our infirmities (Heb. 4:15). He is able to minister to the emptiness in us that has been caused by a broken world. This ministry makes us complete and brings us to wholeness. The wholeness makes it possible to live lives that are restored, renovated, and renewed.

What Do You Do When Your Dream Dies?

If you are like most people, you've had some disappointments along the way, and a few of your dreams have died. Maybe it involved an unfulfilled romance. A lack of parental love. The death of a child. A son or daughter who is trapped in drug or alcohol abuse. A devastating disease or an unexpected divorce. Heartaches happen, no matter who we are or where the course of our life may take us.

> *W*hen God looks for something great to build upon, He looks for ashes.

There are some dreams in my life that cannot be fulfilled. My daddy died. I cannot bring him back. I cannot change the course of childhood. No matter how much I desire the relationship of a natural father, it will not be there. No matter how much I long to be loved by a daddy and to hear him tell me, "You are special," it will not happen. But there have been other blessings, beautiful and unexpected ones.

Part of our ministry is reaching out to thousands of children who come from the inner city. Many of them live in complete brokenness. Far too many do not even know who their father is, much less have a relationship with him. Every week I have the privilege of holding them and hugging them. Randy (a.k.a. "Big Daddy") and I tell them how special they are and how much we love them. Often as I pick up a little girl and minister to her, I am again aware that I am picking up "Paula."

Let me tell you about "T." Randy and I met him years ago when we started this ministry. Each week, we do a one-hour presentation of the gospel from the back of a truck we have driven into a neighborhood. This outreach includes door-to-door visitation the day before our presentation. We are in 65 percent of the government housing projects within our city. One day as I was standing on the truck I heard foul words being yelled at me. Rocks soon began to follow. I ducked as a group of young boys began to hurl whatever they could find to throw.

Hoping to defuse their hostility, I ran over and began to hug them and joke around. And that's when I met "T." For me, he stood apart from the hundreds of other children who were there. Before long, a strong relationship began to develop. We discovered that "T," at the age of ten in modern-day America, could not read. He had been passed from grade to grade, but he remained illiterate. We put him in our academy, especially designed and equipped for children like him.

"T" began to bloom and blossom. He was reading within months. Once told that he would never amount to anything, he was now achieving success. I recall a Sunday evening when "T" went to the altar at church. There he was, bawling like a baby. A concerned elder approached "T" and asked, "What do you want the Lord to do?"

He responded, "I want a daddy; I want to be loved."

My heart bled for him. Oh, how I understood! By God's grace, Randy has become "Big Daddy" to "T," and I have the awesome opportunity of loving him, too.

I might not have had a daddy or the reassurance of love from a father when I was a little girl, but I will make sure that thousands of other children do! God is a God of restoration and resurrection. But He often works through the hearts and hands of people like you and me. What do you do when your dream dies? You let God use you to breathe new life into other people's dreams. As you rejoice with other people, you will find joy enough to fill your own heart as well.

Personal Reflections

Think About This

Read the quotes from this chapter below. After each one take a moment to reflect on how the statement links to a feeling or experience in your own life. Give your own personal reaction to each statement.

1. Pain can become a conduit for power. I eventually discovered that what was meant to destroy us can actually be what makes us strong and whole. What was supposed to be a stumbling block in our lives can actually become a stepping stone. Have you discovered how God turned something destructive in your life into a tool for developing strength and power in your character? How did this happen?

2. When you come to God and offer Him your broken world, you will soon discover that He is the God of restoration. He is the God of renewed hope. He is the God of resurrection. Now describe a work of restoration God has accomplished in your life or in the life of someone you know.

_____

_____

_____

_____

3. What do you do when your dream dies? You let God use you to breathe new life into other people's dreams. As you rejoice with other people, you will find joy enough to fill your own heart as well. Complete this reflective time by describing how you could impact another person's life with the positive message of God's grace and restoration. What steps will you take to complete this gift of hope to that person?

_____

_____

_____

_____

Talk to God

Lord, I give all my disappointments and broken promises to You, for only You can remake my broken world. Remove the self-pity from my heart, and let me see my own hurts as opportunities to make someone else's dreams come true. Help me to under-stand that nothing happens to me without Your approval. Help me to realize that You have promised to take what the enemy has meant for evil and turn it around for my good—and Yours. Right now, I give you the ashes of my life so that You can create a beautiful masterpiece for Your glory. Amen.

SEVEN

New Beginnings

Shortly after I came to know the Lord, God did something amazing and unexpected in my life—He gave me a vision. At the time, I was so new and immature in the things of God that I didn't understand what I had seen. I had no way of realizing that I had received a prophetic vision. It was a long time before I came to see that He was exposing me to the call and destiny of my life.

After worshiping the Lord for many hours in my living room, I had just stretched out on my couch. As I rested there, I saw myself preaching on a mountaintop. There were masses of people surrounding me. As I preached, a mist began to fall on the people, and wherever that mist fell, miracles took place. Some of the listeners fell on their faces, repenting and crying out for salvation. Others were healed. Others had been bound, and I watched as their chains fell off. It was so wonderful!

But there was a multitude of people, and some of those

who were the farthest away could not hear what I was saying. Those who could not hear me fell over the cliffs on the far side of the mountain. As I saw them fall, I wept for them; my heart felt as if it were breaking. Although I was glad for the many who were being so marvelously touched and changed, at the same time I felt tremendously alarmed about those who were falling.

At the end of the vision the Lord said to me, "Preach My gospel." I sat up on the couch feeling both puzzled and petrified. What was I supposed to do? Of course I couldn't preach! Who would listen to me? I had a broken, messed-up past.

As years passed, I still struggled with my history: Could God do anything with a broken person like me who had a tainted past and carried excess baggage? I often wondered, *How can I ever hope to accomplish anything worthwhile in the kingdom of God?*

I have often said, only half kiddingly, that Randy is from five generations of preachers and I am from five generations of heathens. For me, that wasn't really a joke because I couldn't quite see what God would be able to do with a "heathen" woman. I was not raised in church, and unfortunately, I did not hear the gospel until I was almost eighteen years old.

As far as I knew at the time, my life had never been dedicated to God; therefore my actions were not in alignment with God's ways. And the results were self-evident:

> Be not deceived; God is not mocked: for whatsoever a man soweth, that shall he also reap. For he that soweth to his flesh shall of the flesh reap corruption; but he that soweth to the Spirit shall of the Spirit reap life everlasting.
>
> —Galatians 6:7–8

I had sown to the flesh for a lifetime, and there was surely a harvest to be reaped from my actions. What can God do with people who are in the process of harvesting years of junk? I finally found out.

Second Corinthians 5:17 declares, "Therefore if any man be in Christ, he is a new creature: old things are passed away; behold, all things are become new." The Word of God tells us that the moment we say *yes* to Jesus, we become new creatures. A supernatural transformation takes place in the spirit realm.

The moment I came to Jesus, everything "old" passed away, and I became a new person through Christ Jesus. My sins were forgiven, and even better, it was as if I had never committed them in the eyes of God. He not only forgave me, but He forgot about my past. He never brought my past sins up to me or to anyone else. Now, if only I could do the same! In Philippians 3:13–14 we read:

> Brethren, I count not myself to have apprehended: but this one thing I do, forgetting those things which are behind, and reaching forth unto those things which are before, I press toward the mark for the prize of the high calling of God in Christ Jesus.

The apostle Paul reflects in this passage that he has not yet arrived, but there is one thing that is imperative for him to do in order to go forth—*he must forget the past*. He must let go of all his yesterdays. Whether yesterday was good or bad, he must release it.

Like Paul—and like Paula—you cannot enter your tomorrow as long as you hold on to your past. You must let it go.

This is often easier said than done. For many of us, our past not only holds brokenness, disappointment, and scars from life's tragedies, but we are still living out the consequences of our failures and foolish choices. Of course, you would think that letting go of all those bad things would be easy. Yet, often in a twisted, distorted way, we hold on to our past because it is security. It is something with which we are familiar.

Often we are afraid to enter the future because it is unknown and unfamiliar. Even though it may be much better than our past, we have not yet been there. It's unchartered territory. Therefore, we drag the past into our future because somehow it gives us comfort. We feel more comfortable being abased than we do abounding. As long as we continue this way, we cannot be free from the past. And, as Paul admonishes us, how can we go forward if we are always looking back?

What about your past? Are you ready to let it go? Give it a graveyard burial, and do not resurrect it. Your tomorrow does not have to be like your yesterday. In fact, it is a tragedy to plan your future by comparing it to your past! I encourage you from my own experience: Stop using what happened to you in your past to determine what will happen in your future.

God does not necessarily use your past to determine your future, so why should you? Where I came from does not determine where I am going. This is good news for many of us! Too many people have predicted their ending based on their beginning. I am so thankful that God can interrupt a person's life and change the course of history for that person for His good. We see so many examples of this in the Bible. In fact, there are two biblical women who demonstrate this very principle. Let's examine them.

Learning From Ruth

The first woman is Ruth. Apart from the unnamed heroine in Proverbs 31, Ruth is the only lady in the Bible who is called "a virtuous woman." Ruth was born in Moab, and the Moabites worshiped a god by the name of Chemosh. Part of their worship involved sacrificing their own children to this god as an offering. (See 2 Kings 3:27.) This alone tells us that Ruth was raised in a perverse heathen home. She was accustomed to the worst human behavior because the mentality of her people was distorted by their idolatry.

> *S*top using what happened to you in your past to determine what will happen in your future.

Meanwhile, a Jewish farmer and his wife, Naomi, left their home in Bethlehem during a time of famine and relocated in Moab. While in Moab, the couple's two sons married Moabite girls, one of whom was Ruth.

The sons and the father died. The mother-in-law, Naomi, heard that there was no longer a famine back home in Bethlehem, so she decided to return there. She started her journey with her two daughters-in-law. Somewhere along the way, she stopped and told them to turn around and go back to Moab, to return to their people and their gods. One daughter-in-law agreed and chose to go back. But Ruth loved Naomi, and she decided not to return to Moab.

Naomi tried to change Ruth's mind:

> And she said, Behold, thy sister in law is gone back
> unto her people, and unto her gods: return thou after
> thy sister in law. And Ruth said, Entreat me not to
> leave thee, or to return from following after thee: for
> whither thou goest, I will go; and where thou lodgest, I

> will lodge: thy people shall be my people, and thy God
> my God: Where thou diest, will I die, and there will I
> be buried: the LORD do so to me, and more also, if
> aught but death part thee and me.
>
> —RUTH 1:15–17

Ruth recognized that she had already experienced her past, and she hadn't liked it. Her husband had just died, and apparently there was nothing left for her in her former community. Nonetheless, Ruth chose not to be bitter and resentful. Ruth understood the power of choice. She was able to see that we are where we are today because of choices we made yesterday.

Ruth decides to serve Naomi, even though the older woman had grown hard and cynical. When Naomi returned to Bethlehem, she was angry about the death of her husband and sons (Ruth 1:20). When her old friends greeted her by her given name, Naomi, she said, "Don't call me Naomi; call me Mara!" *Mara* means "bitterness," and Naomi was bitter against God. She blamed Him for her losses. In reality, of course, God shouldn't have been blamed. Naomi and her husband had disobeyed Him by going to Moab, and they had suffered the consequences.

Despite Naomi's grudge against Him, God honored Ruth and scheduled Boaz to come into her life. Boaz was one of the wealthiest and most respected men of the city. In time, Boaz and Ruth were married, and they produced a child by the name of Obed, who produced a child by the name of Jesse, who produced a child by the name of David. Their great-grandson was none other than King David, the famous forefather of our Lord and Savior Jesus Christ.

What do we learn from Ruth? We learn that God does not look at where we came from to determine where we are going.

Rahab's Rehabilitation

Another example of a woman's change in direction is found in Joshua, chapter 2. Joshua and the children of Israel were getting ready to possess the land that God had promised them. Joshua sent two spies out to search out the land of Jericho. When the spies arrived in the land, word got back to the king of Jericho, who demanded that the spies be brought before him. To say the least, he probably didn't have their best interests at heart.

Rahab was a harlot who lived in Jericho. The spies were lodging at Rahab's house, and she hid them and protected them from her own king, a courageous act that saved their lives. In turn, when the children of Israel invaded Jericho, they destroyed the city and all of its inhabitants, but they spared Rahab and her family.

Why would this woman of ill repute, a woman who was loose and immoral, be saved? Why didn't God spare some nice little old lady with a white picket fence? Why wasn't a widow or a grandma or a church lady protected instead of a whore? Of all people, why did God save Rahab?

In Joshua 2:9–11 we discover that Rahab had heard about the miracles of the Israelite's God, and she had come to believe that He was the one God. She was acting on that belief when she hid the spies. Rahab heard the word, believed the word, and proved her faith by works (James 2:25). She was saved because of her faith and obedience. Did God want the prostitute? No, but He wanted her faith!

Rahab represents to us the covenant of God. God does not come into covenant with us and use us because we are good people or have a "picture-perfect" past. Nor does God disqualify us because we have a history full of ungodly junk. God comes into covenant with us because of our faith and obedience. Rahab and her family were spared. She later married a "covenant man" and had a child whose son was named Boaz. That's right! Rahab was the grandmother of Boaz, who married Ruth. Think about it. Two women, a pagan and a prostitute, heard and received the covenant of God and became the ancestors of the Lord Jesus Christ.

It bears repeating: God does not need to consult your past to determine your future.

Losing the "Elephant Mentality"

It doesn't matter out of what you have come, what you have done before, or how far you have fallen. God can interrupt your life and change it for His glory—if you will allow Him. Far too many people see themselves as victims of their yesterdays because they have listened to the voice of the enemy. Better they should listen to this: *The devil is a liar!*

Through Christ Jesus, you and I are not victims of our past but victors in our tomorrows. But it is vital that we get rid of the victim, "woe is me" mentality! I can hear someone saying, "But you don't know what I have gone through." Let me share this truth with you. *God has a "now" word to heal the wounds of yesterday.* He is not limited by time. He can go back to your yesterday and be the "balm of Gilead" on its wounds. He can pour out rivers of His healing power all over the abused and rejected little girl inside of your adult body.

Let me ask you to stop right here and answer a very important question: What was it that killed your spirit? What made you bitter? What took the praise out of you? What made you stop believing and hoping? Invite God into that hidden part of yourself right now. Take Him right to the place where you died inside. It might have happened years ago, even decades ago, but God is not limited by time. Allow Him to go back there and to bring healing to your wounded and broken heart. Allow Him to bring closure to memories and wounds that continue to haunt and hurt you.

John 8:36 promises, "If the Son therefore shall make you free, ye shall be free indeed." When Jesus sets you free, *you are free.*

However, far too many of us have what I call the "elephant mentality." Certain elephant trainers use an abusive training strategy when they are preparing elephants to perform in circuses or other shows. The trainer puts massive chains around the baby elephant's feet. Every time the young elephant tries to move forward or run ahead, it is pulled back by the chains and whipped.

The trainers do this until the elephant's spirit is crushed. In other words, they do it until the elephant has been defeated so many times that it will not even make an attempt to move forward. Finally, when that elephant is full grown, they take the chains off. That adult elephant—a massive, mammoth beast—will not run away because it has the painful memory of bondage and beatings.

Isn't that the way we are? We live with such painful memories of the past that we don't have the spirit to move forward. Hurtful or shameful memories can become more real to us than our present reality. The chains have been removed, but we still have the memory of the bondage. We still act as if we are bound, and we walk around with an "elephant mentality." I know, because that's exactly what I did.

Statistics predicted my outcome based on my beginning. Psychiatrists said that I would need counseling for the rest of my life. Having been abused, I was likely to become an abuser. My mind was too infected by sin and sorrow for me to ever become healthy.

I lived with the "elephant mentality" for many years. I was saved from hell, but still bound by the hell of my past. If I took five steps forward, I would feel those old, rusty chains yanking at me, jerking me back ten feet.

One evening I was invited to a dinner party at a lady's home where a missionary/overseer of a particular denomination was also attending. It was a lovely evening. We sat around the pool and listened to adventurous details about life on the mission field. I was in awe of how God could use someone to win so many souls and to change entire nations for His glory. I was even a little envious.

As I listened to this missionary, my heart yearned with desire. By then, years had passed since my vision. That call of God on my life had long been all but forgotten, hidden, and buried in excuses. But now this man suddenly turned to me and began to talk about my future in God. It was as if he knew the secrets God had shared with me. I put my head down and softly began to speak about the vision God had given me. I shared the tragedy of my past as an explanation of why I could not be the one God would use.

That man of God looked at me with piercing eyes and said, "The gifts and calling of God are without repentance" (Rom. 11:29).

The faithful missionary told me that *without repentance* means irrevocable. God does not change His mind when He calls a man or woman of God or places an assignment on his or her life. God is omniscient. He is all-knowing. He knows the past, the present, and the future. It dawned on me that night that if God is all-knowing, He knew every mistake that I would ever make and all the troubles that would occur in my life when He chose to call me. And who can bring judgment against what God had chosen?

It hit me like a ton of bricks! I had been bound with the "elephant mentality." I was free from the past's chains, but I was still bound by their memory. If God could get over my past, who was I not to be able to get beyond it? I was not to hold myself prisoner to my past, nor was I to allow other people in my life to constantly remind me of who I once was and where I had come from.

We must be set free from the opinion of others. Do not allow anyone to hold you to your past. Do not give anybody that opportunity. As Christians, we must develop the attitude that if God has set us free, then who are people to keep us bound? As long as we remain concerned about what people think of us, we are in trouble. We find ourselves on an endless merry-go-round, trying to convince people to like us, accept us, and be pleased with us.

> *If* God could get over my past, who was I or anyone else not to be able to get beyond it?

A quest for the acceptance of people can be disastrous. Often people will suppress you or hold you back to justify their own weaknesses. Let me explain. We are all familiar with the apostle Peter's attempt to walk on water with Jesus (Matt. 14:29). I have heard all kinds of criticism about how Peter began to sink because he had too little faith. But Peter did something that the rest of the disciples failed to do. *He got out of the boat!*

When you get out of the boat, you put the people inside the boat in an awkward position. They must now justify why they are still in the boat. Don't listen to them! It might be lonely on the water, but keep on walking. In the same way, don't allow anyone to hold you back or to make you a prisoner to your past. Remember, you have become a new creation in Christ. Isn't it time you began to see yourself as God sees you?

Abraham's New Life

It is dangerous to hold on to some things that need to be released. We can learn this lesson by considering Abraham's life. (See Genesis 12.) God wanted to establish a nation for Himself, so He chose Abraham to fulfill His purpose and plan. Abraham came from a heathen background. Joshua reveals to us that Abraham and his ancestors served strange gods (Josh. 24:2). But God had His own plans, so He began to tell Abraham that He was going to bless him, make his name great, and establish a nation through his seed. He promised him that his future was going to be much better than his past. And when God began to reveal His plan to Abraham, the first thing He did was to tell Abraham to get out of his country and to get away from his kinfolk.

God showed Abraham what he would inherit once he was willing to leave. The thing that gives us the power to leave one thing is seeing something better that we are going to inherit. If you cannot see that you have a brighter tomorrow, it becomes far more difficult to leave your yesterdays.

When Abraham got ready to leave the "old" to inherit the "new," the Bible records that Lot went with him (Gen. 12:4). Lot was the very thing that God told Abraham to leave! Lot was Abraham's nephew, and God had told him to get away from those crazy kinfolk. There will be some relationships that must be removed from your life before you can inherit the promises that God has for you. We know that eventually Lot caused strife and contention in the life of Abraham. Don't hold on to what should be released in your life. *Some things have to be broken in order for you to be fixed!*

Deliverance Through Worship

There may be things, however, that you don't know how to release. For nearly a year after I received Christ as my Savior, I continued to struggle with bulimia. I would find myself driven to the toilet, hanging over it, and purging myself. Even as I was doing this, I was saying, "God, please forgive me," knowing that I was destroying my body and soul. Before I met Christ, I hadn't felt conviction about my eating disorder. Now I knew it was wrong, but a force beyond myself seemed to be in control.

One particular afternoon, I invited some friends over for a barbecue. After dinner, we began to play Bible Trivia, and before long we began to talk about the goodness of God. I sensed the Spirit of God come into my living room. We soon found ourselves deep in worship.

At some point I left the others and went into my own world of worship. I felt like John, who said, "I was in the Spirit on the Lord's day" (Rev. 1:10). No one laid hands on me, no one prayed with me, but something amazing happened. I was praying in the Spirit in the most intense worship I had ever experienced. Hours passed, but it seemed like minutes. Suddenly, I clearly felt that something that had gripped me from my feet up to my head had been released—something that felt like chains. It was as if a bondage that had held me so tightly had simply fallen away.

Psalm 149:6–9 says:

> Let the high praises of God be in their mouth, and a two-edged sword in their hand; to execute vengeance upon the heathen, and punishments upon the people; to bind their kings with chains, and their nobles with fetters of iron; to execute upon them the judgment written: this honour have all his saints. Praise ye the LORD.

I didn't realize it at the time, but what took place that night is found in this passage. It is saying that when you begin to praise God, the very chains the enemy has used to bind you, the chains that he has wrapped around you, are literally used to wrap around him. That's why the psalmist says, "This honour have all his saints." It is an honor when you begin to praise God and whatever the enemy has used to bind you is cut away from your life. There is deliverance in praise.

That's what happened to me: The bondage of bulimia was broken when I praised God. From that day forth, I never had a desire to purge myself of food again. Also, a true image of myself was restored. Until then I had seen myself as fat even though I was dangerously thin, at times weighing less than eighty pounds. Now I could see myself as I really was. This all took place in a sovereign act of God. I believe that much deliverance takes place through worship.

My deliverance from bulimia came through worship, but my healing and the restoration of my self-image took place through the Word of God and through speaking words of truth to myself.

Words of Hurt, Words of Healing

My mother is now saved, but when I was a young girl she was not a believer, and she was not always wise in her behavior. Shortly after my father's death, I was sitting on the couch with her. She had probably had one or two drinks too many when she looked at me and said, "God, why did You give me such a beautiful little boy and such an ugly little girl?" My brother had always been a handsome boy, while I was, to say the least, destined to become a late bloomer.

Of course, Mom had no intention of damaging my spirit. But her words, which were not wise because of the influence of alcohol, powerfully formed my view of myself. From that point on, it didn't matter who told me I was pretty; I *knew* I was ugly. The enemy used mother's thoughtless words for many years to destroy my self-image.

Too often, the enemy uses words to affect us for the rest of our lives. Haven't you heard some of them? "You are stupid!" "You are so lazy." "What an idiot!" "I swear, you'll never amount to anything!" All these kinds of statements become prophecies that can be, and probably will be, fulfilled unless the Lord intervenes.

Over the course of my life, although she had made that hurtful statement, my mother also told me that I had beautiful hands. She would say, "You have the hands of a piano player. They look like your daddy's hands."

One day the Lord spoke to my heart and said, "Look at your hands and confess aloud that they are beautiful." For weeks I did so. Then He led me to confess the same about my arms and feet. I obeyed. This went on for months, but piece by piece, limb by limb, the Lord gradually brought healing and restoration to my distorted self-image. At last I was able to look in a full-length mirror and say, "Paula, you are a beautiful woman." I finally knew and believed that God had created me in His image, that He had sovereignly chosen the physical traits that make up Paula. I was, therefore, beautiful in His sight. I could have been anyone, but He made me as He did. At last I learned to see myself as God saw me, and in God's eyes I am beautiful.

Do you struggle with self-image? Maybe you are ashamed of your weight or your complexion or your features or your coloring or your proportions. Maybe you hate to go into a room with a mirror. Maybe you think that no one loves you because of the way you look. First, you must accept that God made you who you are. You are beautiful to God! But how can you see yourself as God sees you? I suggest that you find something—maybe just one thing, maybe several—about yourself that you like, then thank Him for it repeatedly. Confess it aloud. Express your gratitude verbally.

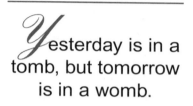

Yesterday is in a tomb, but tomorrow is in a womb.

Thanksgiving is a form of worship, and worship brings deliverance. God wants to deliver you from a poor self-image so that you can see yourself as He sees you. All bondage must be broken. Poor self-esteem must be removed. There are things that God wants released in your life. And as you worship Him and focus on His Word, He will direct you toward freedom. He will help you. Let go of the brokenness of your past. But you have to be willing to release it.

Leaving People, Places, and Things Behind

I have often counseled women who confess that destruction occurred in their life as a result of not leaving something or someone behind. A good friend of mine from California once shared with me her difficulty in serving God because she could not let go of some things. But when she gave her life to the Lord, He instructed her to leave everything behind, to go back to her hometown in Florida, and to leave the relationship that she was in.

Instead of being obedient, this woman tried to justify how she could serve God and minister to those with whom she was involved. She was wrong. Eventually she drifted from her relationship with the Lord and found herself in the same messed-up condition as before.

In God's mercy and grace, He once again reached out to her and restored her broken life. She gave her life over to God, and again, He told her to leave the location and the relationship. This time she packed her bags and ran! Today she has a strong relationship with the Lord and is enjoying a fulfilled life. God does not tell us to do something to frustrate or deprive us; He wants most of all to protect us. He has your best interests at heart. He can see things that you cannot.

When it comes to relationships, I've learned to ask myself this question: "Is this person bringing me closer to God, or is he or she driving me further away?" There are four types of people who will enter your life: those who add, those who subtract, those who multiply, and those who divide. If there are people who are subtracting or dividing in your life, you really need to reevaluate your relationship with them. Maybe they are not God's choice for you.

I have found that one of the greatest reasons for spiritual failure is broken focus. The enemy is a master at sending people, distractions, and things into your life that will take your eyes and focus off God. Beware and take caution. Some things need to be cut out of your life so you can inherit all that God has for you.

There is one important principle that has become vital in my life, and it has to do with releasing the past. What you are intimate with today will be birthed tomorrow. Yesterday is in a tomb, but tomorrow is in a womb. Bury your past and allow intimacy with God to birth His glorious plan for your life!

Personal Reflections

Think About This

Read the quotes from this chapter below. After each one take a moment to reflect on how the statement links to a feeling or experience in your own life. Give your own personal reaction to each statement.

1. What about your past? Are you ready to let it go? Give it a graveyard burial, and do not resurrect it. Your tomorrow does not have to be like your yesterday. Stop using what happened in your past to determine what will happen in your future. On the lines below, write a promissory note to yourself specifying what it is about your past that you will no longer allow to affect your present and future.

_____

_____

_____

_____

2. Thanksgiving is a form of worship, and worship brings deliverance. God wants to deliver you from a poor self-image so that you can see yourself as He sees you. As you worship Him and focus on His Word, He will direct you toward freedom. List some of the characteristics of a poor self-image that you no longer want to affect your thinking so that you can see what God sees in you.

_____

_____

_____

_____

3. The enemy is a master at sending people, distractions, and things into your life that will take your eyes and focus off God. Some things need to be cut out of your life so you can inherit all that God has for you. List the things in your life that you believe God needs to cut away to free you to inherit His destiny.

_____

_____

_____

_____

_____

Talk to God

> *Lord, You are more than able to release me from my past—why should I cling to it? Help me to realize that the blood of Jesus, which was shed on Calvary, is enough to change me from the inside out and that my future need not be determined by my past. Help me to discern what people, places, and things I should leave behind. Break off the chains that bind me as I worship You, and by the power of Your Word destroy every negative word that has been spoken against me. Thank You that You are the God of new beginnings. Amen.*

EIGHT

No More Masks

For the first several years of our marriage, whenever Randy and I fought the aftermath was disastrous. During heated disagreements, Randy would say as little as possible, then he would walk away in order to get his composure and thoughts together. If I had been willing to leave him alone for an hour or two, everything would have been fine. But I wasn't, and I didn't.

Instead, I freaked out whenever he attempted to leave while I was still upset about the disagreement. I didn't care if he wanted to yell at me all night long or if I found myself staring at a blank wall—it didn't matter. He needed to stay right there with me. I wasn't about to let him leave, no matter how bitter the confrontation might have grown.

My reaction to Randy's habit of walking out on arguments caused more than its share of tension between us. When I tried to convince him not to leave me, he would shake his head and say, "Paula, stop being so insecure!"

That made matters ten times worse. In fact, it infuriated me. How dare he say that I was insecure? I carefully pulled on my mask of self-confidence and cited all of the reasons why I *was* secure and why he was the one with the problem. Most of all, I wanted him to know in no uncertain terms how wrong he was to say such a ridiculous thing about me, and how immature he was to walk out in the middle of an argument.

The results were always the same. I was hurt, he was frustrated, and nothing was resolved.

One day I got tired of being on that same merry-go-round ride. I began to cry out to the Lord. In His presence, I ripped off my mask of self-reliance and told Him the truth about my *real* feelings—how insecure I truly was and how deeply I needed His help. When I began to do this, the Lord showed me why I always reacted to Randy in the same way.

The night my father committed suicide, I watched while he fought with my mother over me; I was the pawn between them. After that fight, Daddy left and never came back. With God's help, I suddenly realized that I was bound by fear. Years after my father's death, I was still terrified if Randy walked out in the middle of a disagreement. Why? Because I was so afraid that he would never come back. I somehow thought he would abandon me the way my daddy did.

The moment I was willing to remove my "I'm secure" mask, I was able to identify my real problem. And once I identified it, with God's help I became victorious over it. Randy and I very seldom fight now. But if we do, I give him his space. What's the point in making a scene? He's coming back, anyway.

The Truth of the Matter

When I came to know Jesus, I heard that God was my Father and I was His daughter. I had been adopted, old things had passed away, and all things had become new (2 Cor. 5:17). However, I had not yet figured out how to personalize these truths. I really wanted everything I read about in the Word of God. I wanted to call God "Abba," which also means "Daddy." I wanted to be set free. I wanted to be restored. It was my desire to become everything God intended for me to become, but I had a lot to learn.

Nothing causes us to see what is really inside us like facing a problem under pressure. One day at our church we were having a work day, and everyone had been assigned a particular area of responsibility. There was a young man there that day who had approached my husband several times, asking to join the church staff. As he would with anyone, Randy encouraged him to get "plugged in" so that we could build a relationship with him. We like to know those who labor among us. (See 1 Thessalonians 5:12.)

That afternoon the young man was repairing the church roof. In the process, he touched something that sent a shock to his body. He flew off the ladder, and when he hit the floor, he began to curse like a sailor. Randy rushed over to assist him. Only when he saw Randy did he catch himself and realize what was happening.

Suddenly his language went from "blankety, blank, blank, blank" to "Oh, praise You, Lord, thank You, Jesus!"

What happened? He was under pressure, and pressure brings out what is on the inside of you.

Like this young man, I thought I was victorious until I was put into a pressurized situation. Only then did I discover that I had not overcome; I had simply suppressed. I had learned to hide my weaknesses, insecurities, and failures. I had become a master disguise artist.

I did all this while worshiping in the house of the Lord where there was a certain amount of pressure to live up to an image acceptable in the church. I know that God's Word declares, "Brethren, if a man be overtaken in a fault, ye which are spiritual, restore such an one in the spirit of meekness; considering thyself, lest thou also be tempted" (Gal. 6:1). But I had seen far too many Christians take advantage of people during times of weakness, preying on them like ravenous wolves after wounded sheep. Many times I had seen the strong dominate the weak. For me, the solution was simple—*hide the weakness.*

I have since learned that kind of cover-up is called *hypocrisy.* Does that sound like too strong a word? Just because you have suppressed something, hid it, and pretended it isn't there, should you call that hypocrisy?

Hypocrisy is defined as "pretending to be what one is not." The New Testament meaning of *hypocrisy* and *hypocrite* reflects their use in Greek drama. In the Greek theater, a *hypocrite* was one who wore a mask and played a part on the stage, imitating the speech, mannerisms, and conduct of the character portrayed. Using that definition, a *hypocrite* is simply "one who wears a mask and acts."

No wonder people say that the church is full of hypocrites. We pretend that everything is great when we are hurting and broken. And we sometimes do it because we are afraid not to pretend.

Jesus never had a problem with a hurting and broken person or even with a sinner, but He had all kinds of problems with hypocrites. It amazes me how we have made the church a museum of saints and have forgotten her true mission. It's been said before, but it bears repeating: The church is not supposed to be a museum, but a hospital where the wounded and weak can come in and receive strength, restoration, and healing.

Isn't it time we took off our masks?

As long as I wear a mask, then I am playing the role of a character. And God is not interested in my role-playing or in yours. He wants to deal with you, the *real you!* He wants to know the you that struggles with secret issues of the heart. The you behind the fake smile and pretty clothes. The you that you have to live with every day. The you that wrestles with all sorts of things.

God wants to make you whole. He doesn't want to put a bandage on a broken arm. He wants to reset the bone so there can be proper healing in your life. But for God to minister to us properly, we have to take off our masks and reveal our real needs.

You Cannot Conquer What You Are Unwilling to Confront

Probably the best advice my mother ever gave me came when I was finishing my senior year of high school. By now, you know that I was a mess, and she had good reason to be upset. We were in one of those mother-and-daughter heated discussions because I had made some decisions that were breaking her heart. Like a broken record, she had repeated her speech over and over. It went something like this: "You lie in the bed that you make."

Faced with my "oh-no-here-we-go-again" attitude, my mother was completely frustrated. She blurted out, "You can come in here and fool me, Paula. You can fool your family and your friends, but you'd better be honest with yourself!"

Underneath my sarcastic grin, I knew she was right. She had hit a nerve, and eventually, it proved to be the advice that would change my life.

If I am going to conquer anything in my life, then I must first confront it. Whether it is my past, a character flaw, a weakness, an area of shame, or some unpleasant little secret, to overcome it I must confront it. To confront it, I must be honest about it. I must "own up" to it.

Sometimes this moment of truth is described as "personal insight"—seeing the truth for what it really is, seeing ourselves for who and what we really are. It comes when we get gut-level honest with ourselves. Often we spend great amounts of energy trying to mask our painful inner struggles. Personal insight requires the mask to come off and the role-playing to cease.

> *I*f I am going to conquer anything in my life, then I must first confront it.

We must be like the prodigal son of Luke 15. He had taken all of his inheritance and spent it on wine and women. When he left his father's home, his life began to spin wildly in a downward spiral until he hit rock bottom. At that point, Luke 15:17 records, "And when he came to himself..." The prodigal son had a moment of personal insight: "What have I done? What have I become?"

Isn't it about time you faced your problems, needs, inadequacies, and struggles? Isn't this the perfect day for you to confront yourself with the things you've been hiding? We are far too concerned about getting the speck out of our brother's field of vision when we have a beam protruding from our own eye (Luke 6:41). What we have to confront is the enemy within ourselves. The beginning of transformation takes place when we are willing to make that not-so-easy confrontation.

Facing Hidden Sins

Maybe you aren't struggling with problems, needs, past hurts, or inadequacies. Part of the real you, because you are human, is a sinful nature. And there may be sins in your life that are hidden, that you have masked, that you dare not expose to other Christians or maybe even to yourself. God wants to set you free of those sins, because you cannot experience His best for you when you are living a double life.

Have you been, or are you now, involved with affairs and adulteries or even infatuations with married men? Sometimes when women are desperate for a relationship, unhealthy attractions emerge. The enemy may bring the wrong person along to distract you from God's best. Attractions and affairs with married men will bring pain into your life, and as a child of God, He wants the best for you. Even though you may not be able to see it right now, if you are toying with adultery, you are settling for a VW when God has a Rolls Royce for you.

Have you struggled with lesbianism or homosexual feelings? There are many reasons for a homosexual orientation, but there is no "third gender." God created men men and women women, and it is His will that you be restored to your real, heterosexual self. This may be difficult, but thousands of ex-homosexuals testify that with God's help it is not impossible!

Do you struggle with sins from your past, sins that still haunt you today? Shame and guilt over an abortion, an out-of-wedlock pregnancy, molestation (even though it really wasn't your fault), premarital sex, addictions, substance abuse, and divorce often come between women and God. But this is not God's idea—He has forgiven you; He longs to be in fellowship with you.

> Therefore if any man be in Christ, he is a new creature: old things are passed away; behold, all things are become new.
>
> —2 Corinthians 5:17

You need to identify what you are hiding and what you are using as a mask. You may think that you are not ready, not willing, and even not able to face the "real you." But what you must understand is that God wants to preserve your life. Therefore, He is willing to wrestle with you, to confront you, to have a face-to-face encounter with you. He will meet you in *Peniel* ("the face of God") just as He did with Jacob. (See Genesis 32:30.)

Jacob's "Real Self"

Jacob was the son of Isaac and Rebecca and the twin brother of Esau. From the beginning, even before he was born, we catch a glimpse of his personality type as he wars in the womb to come out first.

> And the Lord said unto her, Two nations are in thy womb, and two manner of people shall be separated from thy bowels; and the one people shall be stronger than the other people; and the elder shall serve the younger. And when her days to be delivered were fulfilled, behold, there were twins in her womb. And the first came out red, all over like an hairy garment; and they called his name Esau. And after that came his brother out, and his hand took hold on Esau's heel; and his name was called Jacob.
>
> —Genesis 25:23–26

Jacob's very name means "heel-catcher, supplanter, cheater, defrauder, and deceiver," and he fit all those descriptions as he grew up. Jacob was a "house boy," a "mama's boy." Esau, on the other hand, was a hunter, a hairy man, physically strong and masculine.

Jacob hung around his mother's dress tail where he learned all of the "tricks of womanhood." From her, he discovered ways to develop his character and nature. Jacob and his mother got together and schemed to steal the birthright that was supposed to be passed on to Esau. This was not necessary, for God had declared to Rebecca that there were two nations in her womb, and that the older would serve the younger. Even before Jacob was born, he was guaranteed to be the ruler.

> When you see God face to face, it cannot fail to produce change in your life.

Many times we are too impatient to wait on the promises of God. That was the reason Rebecca and Jacob took matters into their own hands through manipulation and deception. That was just one of many acts of deception, lying, manipulation, and fraud of which Jacob was a part. Jacob received the birthright, and God blessed him, but he still had that "internal rage" going on inside. That war, that enemy within himself, became the issue with which he and God had to deal.

After stealing the birthright, Jacob fled for his life, fearing what Esau would do to him. He had been living with his uncle Laban for more than twenty years when God told him to return home. On his journey back, he sent word ahead and tried to make peace with Esau. Jacob's messenger returned, telling Jacob that Esau was coming to meet him with four hundred men.

Jacob became extremely distressed, thinking that his brother would most likely kill him. It is at this point in his life that for the first time he got gut-level honest with himself. Praying to God, he confessed for the first time, "I am not worthy of the least of all the mercies, and of all the truth, which thou hast shewed unto thy servant" (Gen. 32:10). Jacob looked inside, reflected, and discovered personal insight. It was from this point of personal insight that he climbs into the wrestling ring with God.

> And Jacob was left alone; and there wrestled a man with him until the breaking of the day. And when he saw that he prevailed not against him, he touched the hollow of his thigh; and the hollow of Jacob's thigh was out of joint, as he wrestled with him. And he said, Let me go, for the day breaketh. And he said, I will not let thee go, except thou bless me. And he said unto him, What is thy name? And he said, Jacob. And he said, Thy name shall be called no more Jacob, but Israel: for as a prince hast thou power with God and with men, and hast prevailed. And Jacob asked him, and said, Tell me, I pray thee, thy name. And he said, Wherefore is it that thou dost ask after my name? And he blessed him there. And Jacob called the name of the place Peniel: for I have seen God face to face, and my life is preserved.
> —GENESIS 32:24–30

There are several truths to learn from this illustration of Jacob's experience.

1. *What you permit will always continue.*

Behavior permitted is behavior perpetuated. Change did not take place until Jacob admitted that there was a problem, a weakness, an area of struggle in his life.

2.   *God will wrestle with you alone.*

God will maneuver you into a place where He can deal with you alone. One of the things that you should both understand and appreciate is that God gives you a season to deal with your issues privately.

3.   *You must want change.*

Jacob told God that he would not let Him go until He blessed him. You must determine that you are not going to continue to live with your condition. Don't get off the surgery table when you begin to feel the pain of the scalpel's cut. Determine that you are not going to run, hide, or pretend. Determine that the thing that has mastered you will finally be defeated through Jesus Christ, and with His help, you will once and for all master it.

4.   *God will wrestle with you to allow you to discover what you are made of.*

God already knows what He created you to be. He knows you intimately, and He knows your ways (Ps. 139:1–3). *He wants you to discover who you are.*

5.   *You must identify your true self.*

God asked Jacob what his name was. Of course, God already knew Jacob's name, but He made Jacob identify himself to admit what his condition was. Jacob had to come to terms with the fact that he was a deceiver, a cheat, and a fraud. Only then did God give him a new name and a new identity.

6.   *You cannot see God face to face until you are willing to see yourself face to face.*

That is why you must take off your mask. Other people might buy into your role-playing deceptions, but not God. He will not sugarcoat the issues in your life, nor will He role-play with you. Jacob had to be willing to come clean and to deal with his issues in order to see God face to face. And when you see God face to face, it cannot fail to produce change in your life.

7. *God will wrestle with you until you face the facts of your life and deal with them.*

He is asking you right now, "Who are you, really?" He wants you to deal with your mask so He can deal with your condition. He is demanding that you offer Him your true self, baggage and all, so that He may preserve your life and restore you.

Discovering True Confession

I recall doing my first television interview. I was asked to be a guest on a show that would focus on the topic of evangelism. I went to the studio with great anticipation and eagerness to share what God was doing in the inner city where Randy and I were pastors. Little did I know that God would climb into the wrestling ring with me on that day, television audience and all.

In the middle of the interview, the host stopped and asked me why I do what I do. I knew why. I was ministering to a little "Paula" every time I picked up a hurting child. But no one else knew. I had concealed it well, behind a "perfect Christian" mask. Now, unexpectedly, I suddenly began to tell it all, from my father's suicide to the abuse and rejection.

Up until the time of that interview, I had been deeply ashamed of my past, fearful that if people knew about it, they would not receive me. But as I began to speak it forth, a tremendous healing began to take place. Now I understand why Revelation 12:11 states that we overcome Satan by the blood of the Lamb and the word of our testimony. With every word that I spoke forth, I was overcoming!

There is such power in confession.

> Confess your faults one to another, and pray one for another, that ye may be healed. The effectual fervent prayer of a righteous man availeth much.
>
> —JAMES 5:16

The Word of God tells us that we are healed, or made whole, when we confess our weaknesses, faults, and struggles. It actually strengthens me to acknowledge my weakness.

A couple of warnings are in order. First of all, God does not want us to continue in sin—but He wants to restore sinners. Let's make it clear that sin *does* separate us from God, but that God desires intimacy in His relationship with you. That's why John wrote to us and said, "My little children, these things write I unto you, that ye sin not. And if any man sin, we have an advocate with the Father, Jesus Christ the righteous: And he is the propitiation for our sins: and not for ours only, but also for the sins of the whole world" (1 John 2:1–2).

God wants you to be in fellowship with Christians who will love you, support you, pray for you, and stand with you while you are in the process of being transformed.

Second, when there is need to confess a fault or failure, be careful to whom you make your confession. Make sure that your friend is trustworthy, prayerful, mature, godly, and able to keep your confidence. If you are in a church or Bible study environment where you will be criticized for your struggle with some particular weakness, fault, or sin, leave and find another one. God wants you to be in fellowship with Christians who will love you, support you, pray for you, and stand with you while you are in the process of being transformed. Galatians 6:1–2 says:

> Brethren, if a man be overtaken in a fault, ye which are spiritual, restore such an one in the spirit of meekness; considering thyself, lest thou also be tempted.

David said:

> For I acknowledge my transgressions: and my sin is ever before me. Against thee, thee only, have I sinned, and done this evil in thy sight: that thou mightest be justified when thou speakest, and be clear when thou judgest. Behold, I was shapen in iniquity; and in sin did my mother conceive me. Behold, thou desirest truth in the inward parts: and in the hidden part thou shalt make me to know wisdom.
> —PSALM 51:3–6

David admonishes us to acknowledge our weaknesses, struggles, and sin. Own up to it!

Every time a healing has taken place in my life, there has been one common denominator: I had to stop pretending and take off my mask, identifying and confessing the condition. Once those things took place, healing followed.

How about you? Don't continue to role-play or hide behind some hypocritical mask. Allow God to wrestle with you. He wants you to tell Him who you really are and what your condition really is. He wants to give you a new identity—the one of His choosing. Above all else, He wants to make you whole.

Personal Reflections

Think About This

Read the quotes from this chapter below. After each one take a moment to reflect on how the statement links to a feeling or experience in your own life. Give your own personal reaction to each statement.

1. Isn't it about time you faced your problems, needs, inadequacies, and struggles? Isn't this the perfect day for you to confront yourself with the things you've been hiding? The beginning of transformation takes place when we are willing to make that not-so-easy confrontation. On the lines below, honestly list the hidden issues that you try to hide—even from God.

_____

_____

_____

_____

_____

2. On pages 125–127, the author lists seven truths from the illustration of Jacob's struggle with God at Peniel. Read these seven truths again, and then list the three that represent the areas of your greatest struggle with your past. Tell how these three truths can help you take off your mask and deal once and for all with your past.

(1) _____

(2) _____

(3) _____

Talk to God

> *Lord, help me to identify those things that are holding me back or keeping me from becoming all You desire me to be. Help me to stand before You fully exposed, without a costume or a mask to hide the things that shame me. I want to deal with the sins and other issues in my life that I continue to wrestle with, for I cannot conquer what I'm unwilling to confront. So right now, I bring before You the following things:*

_____

_____

_____

> *Lord, I am determined to allow You to change me. Please begin right now. Amen.*

NINE

Imagery and Imagination

Across the screen moves the beautiful prostitute who is about to be swept off her feet and rescued from her gutter lifestyle. Her savior is a multimillionaire, who also happens to be an extremely handsome, charming, kind, sensitive, romantic, and funny man. The film, *Pretty Woman*, starring Julia Roberts and Richard Gere, is a modern-day fairy tale. Years after its release, the movie is still a popular one.

Why is it such an all-time favorite film? For one reason, when we women get a little discouraged, we can just remember that Julia Roberts went from the pit to the palace when her knight in shining armor fell in love with her. The movie fills us with hope and anticipation: Surely something like that will be the turning point of our lives, too. But in reality we are often left with this question: "Why hasn't anyone brought me my glass slipper yet?"

Our Unending Search for Love

It is the heart cry of every woman to be loved. But if we do not discover, understand, and accept the love of God, then we cannot discover and love ourselves. And if we do not love ourselves, then we cannot love others. We cannot give what we do not have. It is impossible to give something that we do not possess. How can we love someone else if we don't love ourselves? And how can we love ourselves if we never understand how valuable we are or realize that we are fearfully and wonderfully made?

> I will praise thee; for I am fearfully and wonderfully made: marvellous are thy works; and that my soul knoweth right well.
>
> —Psalm 139:14

Many women spend their lives suffering from low self-esteem, an inferiority complex, and insecurity because they never understand their value. They do not see themselves as God sees them. With an improper image of yourself, it is nearly impossible to receive the good things that God has for you. You will think you are not worthy, not deserving, and not a candidate for God's goodness.

An improper image of yourself will distort your view and misalign you with your blessings, rendering you unable to receive all that God has for you. He has good things for you, not just spiritually but in every area of your life. God has good things for you in your emotions, body, finances, and relationships. God wants you to be complete in every area. It is His will for *you*, not just for Suzy or Jane or Amanda. God's best for you is attainable; it's not just a faint and distant hope.

Problems occur in women's lives when the desire for love remains unmet. We become vulnerable when we pursue love in the wrong manner. Desire creates pursuit. What I want, I go after. That is why God so carefully told us to "delight thyself also in the LORD; and he shall give thee the desires of thine heart" (Ps. 37:4). He is saying to put Him first so our desires will be in the proper proportion to His will for our lives.

God knows better than anyone that we always will pursue what we desire. The more we want something, the more we will go after it. The magnitude of our craving will determine the extent of our pursuit. As women, we have been created to desire love above all things. This desire fulfilled by the wrong relationship or pursued in the wrong way can become disastrous in our lives. Think of all the crazy things you have done in the pursuit of love. (If you're like me, you'd rather not!) Think of the extremes you have gone to. Think of the sacrifices you've made.

Our desire for love is not wrong in itself, but our search for it often takes us in the wrong direction. We live in a culture and society that bombard us with "fantasy living." Romance novels are still the bestsellers. Daytime soap operas hold millions of women captive with their steamy, seductive "love plots." We are fascinated with the latest juicy news on Hollywood's Tinseltown couples.

We create "superhumans" out of movie stars and celebrities and stand in awe of their every move. We don't want to know about their flaws and imperfections, which would taint the image and mar the fantasy. Fans spend billions of dollars for tickets to the latest box-office hit. Movies promise pleasure, not just for two hours of viewing, but by providing a lingering memory that somehow allows us to live the part of some glamorous, brilliant, or otherwise desirable character. We are mesmerized by a fantasy world in which we try to scriptwrite our own lives.

There are some grave dangers, however, in scriptwriting our

lives, particularly as a fantasy or a romance. A fantasy is the product of our imagination or mood. And we ought to know by now how quickly moods can change. Chances are, what you were in the mood for a few years ago doesn't appeal to you today. For that matter, what you were in the mood for a week ago probably doesn't entice you right now.

Emotions: A Poor Compass

I cannot make "life decisions" based solely on how I feel. My feelings cannot be the compass that directs my steps in life. If they are, I will remain in a whirlwind of confusion, because my feelings change constantly. The Bible lets me know in no uncertain terms that my steps are supposed to be ordered by the Lord, not by my emotions.

> The steps of a good man are ordered by the LORD: and he delighteth in his way.
>
> —PSALM 37:23

Emotions can be deceptive. How can I trust in something that is not always truthful? And as far as imagination is concerned, it is God who gave it to us in the first place, so imagination, in and of itself, is not bad. However, it must be nurtured properly with perimeters and control. There is a huge difference between fantasy and God's dream for your life. What distinguishes and sets them apart from each other is their source. The Bible explains:

> For the weapons of our warfare are not carnal, but mighty through God to the pulling down of strong holds; casting down imaginations, and every high thing that exalteth itself against the knowledge of God,

and bringing into captivity every thought to the obedience of Christ.

—2 Corinthians 10:4–5

A fantasy stems from a desire rooted in the flesh. God's dream for you stems from a desire rooted in His Spirit. We are not instructed to quit imagining, but to destroy every imagination or thought that is contrary to God and His will for our lives. We are to take every thought prisoner by seizing it and leading it into captivity to obey Christ.

An improper image of yourself will distort your view and misalign you with your blessing, rendering you unable to receive all that God has for you.

Obviously, there is a battle going on in my mind. The Bible's strong terminology suggests I am being bombarded with thoughts that will lead me astray and produce destruction in my life. The problem is not that I am not to imagine, for it will take imagination to produce the dream of God in my life. But I am to fight off the imaginations that will lead me into fantasy living and into daydreams that are contrary to God's purpose and plan for my future.

Women fantasize because of lack in our lives. I reason that if something is missing in my life, then maybe I can live it out in your life—even if in reality you are not the person that I have imagined you to be. It is my own lack or void that I am trying to fulfill. It is easier to fulfill this through a fantasy than through reality. *Fantasy* is, in essence, the mentality of "why hasn't anyone brought me my glass slipper yet?"

Fantasy is much more appealing than reality because, in our minds, satisfaction always comes easy. It is the "perfect plot" with the "perfect me," the "perfect him," and the "perfect place." It happens with such natural ease. But let me interrupt your thoughts right now and bring you back to reality. It is not true that there cannot be a fairy-tale story in your life. But it won't come easily—your "happily ever after" is going to take a lot of work and a willingness to go through great opposition to get it. You are going to have to be willing to fight to lay hold of every promise God has for you.

Fighting for the Promise

I often reflect on Numbers 13, in which the children of Israel have been promised Canaan, a land that flows with milk and honey. It was their Promised Land, but as you already know, there were giants standing in the way, hindering Israel's attainment of the promises. As we discovered in an earlier chapter, many people are discouraged or intimidated by the giants that stand between them and their promises. Sometimes they revert to fantasies instead of fighting the giants.

First of all, we need to recognize that the giants are usually signposts that we are getting closer and closer to the land of promise. To inherit the land, we have to fight the giants. To possess the promise, we must be willing to deal with the problem. The apostle Paul admonished us:

> Fight the good fight of faith, lay hold on eternal life, whereunto thou art also called, and hast professed a good profession before many witnesses.
> —1 TIMOTHY 6:12

Paul is saying that if we are going to inherit the promises of heaven, we must fight the good fight. Don't let God's promises pass you by because you are unwilling to confront the opposition!

Family Fantasies

It is precisely when we refuse to face our giants that we begin to live vicariously through the lives of others. Whether it is through soap operas, romance novels, movies, or even our children or our spouse, we choose to play a part and live it out. While on a plane, I saw a documentary of Princess Diana's life. The producers had interviewed people from all over the world about their reactions to her death. People were crying with such heartfelt affection for the princess that it was as if it were their own sister or daughter who had died. They called her the "People's Princess." One lady who was interviewed concurred with what many others felt—she had lived her own fairy-tale dream through the life of Princess Diana. She said, "I was a princess through her."

> *We* are not instructed to quit imagining, but to destroy every imagination or thought that is contrary to God and His will for our lives.

It's not only celebrities about whom we fantasize. I cannot tell you how many times I have seen parents push their children to extremes, not for the sake of the children but to live out their own unfulfilled dreams.

My son played football. The kids were great, but some of the parents were totally out of control. At the games, I saw mothers reliving unfulfilled childhood dreams through their little girls, whom they were pushing into the role of cheerleaders against the children's wishes. I saw men who were seeking to find a sense of fulfillment through their sons. It is OK to encourage our children and even to stretch them. But danger occurs when we try to "live through them." When this takes place, we often make demands on them that they cannot fulfill. They in turn become miserable, which eventually makes us miserable, too.

We don't always stop with our children. How many women watch some hot love scene in a movie and then carry home an artificially inspired erotic desire into their own bedrooms? Before they realize it, they are staring at the eight-inch love handles on their husband's sides, wondering what happened to the solid-rock pectoral muscles and chiseled-down waist they just saw on the big screen.

These same women are frustrated when they fail to find roses strewn all over the bed, along with candles and music to set the mood, placed there by a devoted spouse. Fantasy has begun to interfere with reality, and before they know it, they forget why they fell in love and married that man sleeping next to them in the first place. Fantasy living demands unrealistic expectations, and when expectations are not met, they cause frustration. Frustration in a marriage or relationship can lead to isolation. Isolation can lead to separation, and ultimately, to divorce.

If your relationship is being measured against a "fantasy" yard-stick, then you need to find a new standard of measurement! Go back in your mind and remember what it was that made you fall in love with your man in the first place. If there is only one quality you can find in him that you admire today, then focus on that quality. Thank God for it. Mention it over and over to your-self—and to him. Stop telling him all the things you dislike; tell him what you *do* like about him. Don't throw away your promises to chase some elusive dream.

"If Only" Fantasies

Another danger of fantasy living is "if only" thinking, which causes us to procrastinate. A fantasy always awaits the "right" or "perfect" occasion. It holds us trapped in a time warp, saying "if only," and waiting for the "right" time. James declares, "Whereas ye know not what shall be on the morrow. For what is your life? It is even a vapour, that appeareth for a little time, and then vanisheth away" (James 4:14). Life is here, then it is gone. It passes very quickly.

Fantasy living causes us to put off until tomorrow what we should do today. We make excuses:

- *If only* my kids were grown, then I could start that important, God-inspired ministry.

- *If only* I had enough money, then I would begin that new business...or have that first baby.

- *If only* I had more time, then I would write that first book.

- *If only* he would change, then I would love my husband.

We say we'll do this or do that when such and such is in order. But "such and such" will never be in order, because the enemy will see to it that we never have a perfect opportunity. Please don't wait until everything is perfect to pursue the promises of God in your life. Go for it in the middle of a mess! Otherwise, your life will have passed you by, and you will have never accomplished God's destiny.

Another danger of "fantasy living" is that you could spend your whole life trying to be someone else instead of who you were created to be. If you never get an understanding of who you are in Christ—that He loves you for who you are—then you can never fulfill His purpose for you. Instead, you live out your life as an impostor, which is a very unfulfilling role. It is your uniqueness that separates you and makes you special.

> *D*on't let God's promises pass you by because you are unwilling to confront the opposition!

Look at your hands right now. There is no one in this entire world that has your set of fingerprints. You are unique and unduplicated in all creation. Those one-of-a-kind marks at your fingertips set you apart to do what only you can do. You need to understand that your value is found in your *difference* from everyone else, not in your *similarity*. I cannot overemphasize this enough. Understand the value of your uniqueness. Realize that when you get saved, God does not change your personality—He changes your character.

For many years, I lived in a fantasy world, pretending, hoping, comparing, neglecting, and even self-destructing. When I finally came to terms with my real self, I had to make the transition into a new life through trust in the God who created me. When it all boiled down to it, the question was very simple: "Does God really love me? Or doesn't He?" The answer changed my life forever, and it will change yours, too, once you accept it, once you believe it, and once you begin to live in its wonderful truth.

Personal Reflections

Think About This

Read the quotes from this chapter below. After each one take a moment to reflect on how the statement links to a feeling or experience in your own life. Give your own personal reaction to each statement.

1. The Bible's strong terminology suggests I am being bombarded with thoughts that will lead me astray and produce destruction in my life. The problem is not that I am not to imagine, for it will take imagination to produce the dream of God in my life. But I am to fight off the imaginations that will lead me into fantasy living and into daydreams that are contrary to God's purpose and plan for my future. What are the imaginations and fantasies that do not line up with God's purpose and plan for your life?

_____

_____

_____

_____

2. The author makes the following statement: "Fantasy living causes us to put off until tomorrow what we should do today. We make excuses." What are the "excuses" that you have made by indulging in the "if only" fantasies that you have entertained in your mind?

_____

_____

_____

_____

3. Another danger of "fantasy living" is that you could spend your whole life trying to be someone else instead of who you were created to be. Understand the value of your uniqueness. Realize that when you get saved, God does not change your personality—He changes your character. Complete this reflective step by listing the ways in which God has changed your character. Take time to carefully explain how your character has changed with God's help.

_____

_____

_____

_____

_____

_____

_____

Talk to God

> *Lord, if I have allowed my imagination to create a false future or if I have created a script for my life that is not Your will for me, please forgive me. Cleanse me from ideas that have come into my mind through films, movies, music, and other ungodly influences. I know that Your plans for me are bigger and more wonderful than anything I could plan for myself, so help me to keep my heart set apart to produce Your plans for me. Teach me to trust You with my relationships, with my responsibilities, and with my desires; help me to bring every thought captive to the obedience of Christ. Amen.*

TEN

Because I Love You

Once I came to know the Lord, I prayed fervently and continually for my family. Finally, after several years, my mother experienced a dramatic conversion through Christ Jesus. Not long afterwards, I was at Mom's kitchen table talking about God's sovereignty over our lives. We reflected on the past, on my father's death, and on his family. Tears began to well up in Mom's eyes. She whispered, "You know, Paula, Mama Annie was a very religious woman."

"Mama Annie was religious? I had no idea." I looked at Mom in surprise.

After I went to bed, I couldn't get Mama Annie off my mind that night. As I remembered her, the Lord revealed to me how His love had been there—unseen and unrecognized—from the beginning of my life. Many of my relatives had rejected me for their own reasons. But Mama Annie had always loved me dearly. Even as a tiny child I had somehow felt that I was her favorite. Despite her painful battle with rheumatoid arthritis and all her other diffi-culties, genuine love had always shone through her eyes.

All at once a faint memory became increasingly clear. I was warmed to the heart thinking back upon how she had held me and rocked me in her arms. I recalled her mumbling what I thought was gibberish. All at once I understood that she had been praying in the Spirit, asking God's blessing on me.

I believe that when I was only a baby, Mama Annie dedicated me to the Lord. And I believe today that the words she spoke over me back then established the will of God in me and confirmed His destiny over my life. Today I am able to see that His hand-prints were there all along. As much as the enemy tried to destroy me, God had a different plan. He had a sure covenant with me.

The most glorious day of my life took place when I entered that trailer home and was introduced to the Son of God, whom I made my Lord and Savior. I had a divine appointment and didn't even know it. Isn't that how God works? He puts us at the right place at the right time to set us up with our divine destiny. We have very little to do with most of the blessings in our lives. God simply orders and directs our footsteps all along the way.

My unexpected meeting with Jesus was a day of destiny for me. My life would be changed, forever. It was the first day of a process in which, layer by layer, all of the wounds, hurts, rejec-tion, and betrayal of my past were peeled away. Even today, He continues to restore me through His love, mercy, and grace. This process allowed me to discover God and to become intimate with Him. That, in turn, allowed me to discover myself and find the love that I had always longed for.

With each step of the process the Spirit of God wrapped His

arms of love around me. He walked me through the journey. He helped me die to old habits and ways of thinking. He enabled me to discover who God isn't, so that I could understand who He is. He forgave the unforgivable, delivered me from my past, and gently removed my masks so I could finally be myself. He removed my empty fantasies, and like a master sculptor creating a fine piece of art, He replaced them with a carefully designed life that continues to demonstrate His workmanship.

The enemy had attempted to blind me and keep me from the love of God. He tried to distort my view of love through damaged relationships so I could never crawl up in my heavenly Father's lap and cry out "Abba, Father, Daddy!" But he has been defeated!

Just as His love did for me, God's love is able to reach into the deepest pit of your life, pull you out of your mess, and set you on the solid rock. He is able to heal your heart, even if it has been broken and shattered into a million pieces. He is able to take the ashes of your life and create beauty. He is able to provide for you a safe and secure environment in a mean and cruel world. He is able to be your Superman, your hero. He is not just able, but He is also ready and willing to do so because He wants so much for you to know that He loves you.

> The LORD hath appeared of old unto me, saying, Yea, I have loved thee with an everlasting love: therefore with lovingkindness have I drawn thee.
> —JEREMIAH 31:3

Throughout ten thousand millenniums, eons before He formed the earth and everything in it, God has always loved you. He has always had you on His mind. I did not realize it for a long time, but God's love was always there. In the middle of my messed-up world,

God's grace and love were drawing me to Him, even though I could not always clearly hear and distinguish His voice.

God's Overpowering Love

Some of us should not be alive and well today. There may have been events in your life that could have wiped you out. Maybe you should have lost your mind. Perhaps you ought to be dead. But the devil is a liar, and God has a far different plan for you than destruction. He has reached down to you in love, mercy, and grace, and He has made a way to rescue you.

But maybe you don't feel rescued. Maybe you are still struggling with feelings of sorrow and abandonment. What has distanced you from receiving God's love? Has someone betrayed you and broken your heart into a million pieces? Have you thought that you could never get over "him" walking out and telling you he never really loved you in the first place? Have you hated other women because of past unkindness and disappointment? Have you struggled with failure and weakness so long that you think God could never forgive you, much less love you? Have you been so unloved by people—perhaps by a father or a husband—that you cannot imagine God loving you deeply, dearly, and unconditionally?

God's love is able to reach into the deepest pit of your life, pull you out of your mess, and set you on the solid rock.

No matter what you've been through, no matter what seems to be blocking the way between you and God, nothing can prevent His loving You. God is working in your life and on your behalf so that you can discover the love He has for you. When you do discover it, you will understand the beautiful promise given below:

> Who shall separate us from the love of Christ? Shall tribulation, or distress, or persecution, or famine, or nakedness, or peril, or sword? As it is written, For thy sake we are killed all the day long; we are accounted as sheep for the slaughter. Nay, in all these things we are more than conquerors through him that loved us. For I am persuaded, that neither death, nor life, nor angels, nor principalities, nor powers, nor things present, nor things to come, nor height, nor depth, nor any other creature, shall be able to separate us from the love of God, which is in Christ Jesus our Lord.
> —ROMANS 8:35–39

Once you experience God's love for yourself, you will understand that no thing, no being seen or unseen, no situation, no circumstance, no attack—absolutely *nothing*—can separate you from the love of God.

Joseph: A Life of Losses

The Old Testament character Joseph (with his coat of many colors) went through more trouble than most of us could have endured. (His story starts in Genesis 37.) At the beginning of his life, he received the birthright blessing, yet he was born into a broken world. He was the object of his brothers' jealousy and hatred. Through their cruelty, he was separated from his family and from his father whom he loved. His mother died. He was sold into slavery and ended up in a strange land. He was falsely accused by a spiteful woman and thrown in prison. He thought he would never get out.

Joseph's world was shattered, and he suffered psychological and emotional trauma as a result. How do I conclude that? Because when his brothers, who had sold him into slavery, finally came to Egypt to find food and Joseph saw them, he played a little head game with them. He disguised himself and wasn't able to face them. Why? If you have ever really been hurt, it is hard to face your assailants. Eventually, however, he was reunited to his father and family.

On his deathbed, Joseph's father Jacob spoke God's Word over his beloved son:

> Even by the God of thy father, who shall help thee; and by the Almighty, who shall bless thee with blessings of heaven above, blessings of the deep that lieth under, blessings of the breasts, and of the womb: The blessings of thy father have prevailed above the blessings of my progenitors unto the utmost bound of the everlasting hills: they shall be on the head of Joseph, and on the crown of the head of him that was separate from his brethren.
>
> —Genesis 49:25–26

Joseph still had some blessings coming to him. Although he was a powerful prime minister, although he had the big house, the money, and the wife, there were still some things that Joseph needed. He needed emotional and psychological healing, and there was some healing still coming out of heaven for the pain he had endured. And if this was true for Joseph, it's true for you: *After you pass through pain and sorrow, God will always appoint a time of healing and restoration for you.*

God's Messengers of Love

From the time I was first saved, I heard that God loved me so much that He gave His only begotten Son. I was told that if I believed on Him, I would not perish but have everlasting life (John 3:16). But as often as I heard this amazing information, I didn't comprehend it. I couldn't see that God was working in my life and on my behalf to acquaint me with His unconditional love. It took years for me to understand that He loves me "just because," not because I am a "good" girl. He doesn't love me because I deserve it or have earned it. He doesn't love me because I first loved Him. He loves me just because He is God and just because I am His daughter.

I want to take a close look at one particular word that Paul uses in the Book of Ephesians. He writes:

> That Christ may dwell in your hearts by faith; that ye, being rooted and grounded in love, may be able to comprehend with all saints what is the breadth, and length, and depth, and height; and to know the love of Christ, which passeth knowledge, that ye might be filled with all the fulness of God.
> —EPHESIANS 3:17–19

The word *to know* in the original Greek language means "to feel." That kind of knowing takes us beyond intellectual knowledge and reaches into our hearts. God wants to instill His love in us so that we not only acknowledge it but experience it. God desires to be intimate with you, so much so that the Song of Solomon illustrates His passionate love for His bride—and you are His bride. God will woo you. He will draw you to Himself. He is in love with you.

God has demonstrated His love for me again and again. Every time I begin to feel unworthy, or assume that I don't really deserve the love of God because of my old ways of thinking, God pours out His love in abundance. He has revealed His love in many different ways. His tender mercies come from all directions, and He often works through people. But the loving message has only one source: God Himself.

The moment I met Him, God began to do a quick work to demonstrate His love and character in my life. He used special messengers to communicate with me. I started attending a small church, and three elderly women took an interest in me. They encouraged me to immerse myself in the Word of God. They called me often and taught me about the Christian life. They bought me tapes to listen to and books that would help me with my spiritual growth. They invited me to pray with them, and they took me by the hand, walking with me as they prayed. They were very sincere and pure in their love for God, and I was being discipled by them without even knowing it. God was demonstrating His love to me through these ladies.

God has also used Randy to express His love for me. God has brought healing and restoration through Randy and has used him to help me confront my past. He has used him to model for me the power of forgiveness. He has used Randy to help bring healing to me sexually and to teach me intimacy without fear. He has used him to restore belief that all men are not bad and that they will not all abandon me or hurt me. He has used him to make me see and obey the call of God on my life. He has used the Christlikeness in my husband to help me understand the safety that comes through submission. He has used him to demonstrate that love is not a feeling but a commitment.

Because I Love You

I remember one confrontation between us that taught me more about love than I could ever have learned any other way. I was trying to make Randy say what I wanted to hear. In other words, I was attempting to manipulate him. Suddenly he turned and pointed his finger right in my face. His expression was an unforgettable combination of love and compassion. He said, "Paula, you cannot push me away; I am going to grow old with you, *because I love you.*"

I jumped up and ran out of the room. I felt as if someone had literally poured liquid fire all over me. For the first time in my life, I fully experienced the power of unconditional love. I was not used to this. I was accustomed to pushing people out of my life before they could hurt me. But Randy White was going nowhere. Even though I was frustrating him, his love for me was not diminishing but growing stronger every day. When I ran out of the room, I was crying intensely, overwhelmed by what I was feeling and experiencing. Suddenly the Lord whispered to my spirit, "Randy is My gift to you, because I love you."

Right after the Los Angeles riots of 1993, God allowed me to go into the inner city of Los Angeles. Anyone in his right mind was trying to get out of Los Angeles, but God was sending me in there. He planted me directly in the heart of the riot-stricken area. We were on the streets for over thirteen weeks and saw tens of thousands of people born again into the kingdom of God.

Since then, I've traveled and preached the gospel all over the world. Thousands upon thousands of people have been born again, and the Spirit of God has been poured out in an unprecedented fashion in crusades across America and through my nationally syndicated TV program, *Paula White Today*. I have studied the great revivals of old, and I knew that I was in the midst of one of the greatest outpourings of God's Spirit. I was able to minister with God's generals and commanders in chief. I saw the miraculous—I was there when it happened. I cannot begin to tell you how humbling and awesome it is that God has given me such amazing opportunities to see His work in the world.

What a privilege it is to lead someone to the saving knowledge of Christ. I went back to my hotel room one night after the "glory cloud" of the Lord had literally appeared. For hours we had basked in the presence of God. Some had cried; others had laughed. Many ran to the altar, repenting and confessing Jesus as their Lord and Savior without anyone giving a formal invitation. Miracles, signs, and wonders had occurred. I knew God could allow anyone this opportunity, yet He had chosen me. In my room I sat still in the presence of God, my heart overflowing with gratitude. His voice softly whispered, "This is My gift to you, Paula, because I love you."

> *This is My gift to you, Paula, because I love you.*

When Randy and I left Washington, D.C. and came to Tampa, we left everything behind and simply lived by faith. When we started the great church that we now pastor, we went without any salary for over a year. This was something between the Lord and Randy and me. I believe that a man and woman of God are worthy of double honor or pay according to the scriptures (1 Tim. 5:17). But this was a unique season in our life. There were nights when Randy would hold me and say, "These will be the best days of our life." But on more than one occasion, I opened the refrigerator door and began to prophesy food into the empty shelves. I know what it is to roll pennies when you are right in the middle of God's will. During this season, God never failed us or disappointed us. He sustained us and supernaturally blessed us. It is absolutely God's will to bless His children, and He wants us to bless each other.

Randy and I have learned to live out the principles of Luke 6:38:

> Give, and it shall be given unto you; good measure, pressed down, and shaken together, and running over, shall men give into your bosom. For with the same measure that ye mete withal it shall be measured to you again.

We have come to understand the principles of giving and receiving God's harvest. I love to give. It is one of my greatest joys in life. When I give in abundance over and beyond my tithe, I see God's harvest in abundance (2 Cor. 9:6).

However, I found it to be much easier to give than to receive. A man of God spoke words of wisdom into my life when he told me that people have a difficult time receiving because they lose control. When you give, you have control. When you receive, you don't. When God began to bless us, one of the things He gave us was a beautiful home. For days I walked around thinking, *Oh, I shouldn't have this. Something is wrong with this picture—it's just too good to be true.* I struggled with receiving God's blessing until one night when I was sitting in my bathtub. Out of nowhere, I heard the Lord whisper, "This is My gift to you, because I love you."

Learning to Love God's Women

God has done a powerful work of healing in me through the power of His love. In every area of my life, He continues to work, bringing restoration and wholeness. When we first began our church, God directed me to start a women's ministry. My initial reaction was, "Oh no, You must have the wrong person." I still had some lingering bad effects from my previous encounters with hurtful girls and women, and I wasn't at all interested in trying to minister to a group of them.

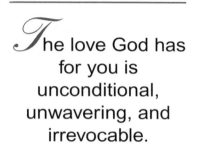

The love God has for you is unconditional, unwavering, and irrevocable.

But God was persistent, and He continued to lay a burden on me for a ladies' ministry. Gradually, my heart was turned toward them, and I found myself with a real desire to see them healed and made whole. But I still did not know how to interact very well with women.

Once I realized that this was a challenge, God spoke three things to my spirit:

1. Fill the women with the Word of God.

2. Build godly relationships through fellowship.

3. Spoil them, pamper them, and shower them with "good things."

He made these three things extremely clear to me. Why? Because He wanted to demonstrate His love to other women in the same way He had demonstrated it to me. It was really quite a challenge.

Apart from the three elderly mentors who first discipled me, I'd never had really healthy relationships with women. I had women acquaintances, but not solid friendships built on love and trust. As it turned out, God brought restoration to me in that area as I obeyed what He asked of me. He has since brought into my life some very special women who have become true friends and armorbearers.

Not only have I been able to befriend and minister to each lady in our fellowship, but every woman who God has brought into my life has helped to complete me in some way. We are all different from each other and yet so alike. For years we have met together each week. Some ladies are serious and speak into my life. Some pray and intercede for me with such fervency that you'd think I was their own daughter or sister. Others just make me laugh. Like a colorful puzzle, God has designed each one of us to fit together to form His beautiful picture.

> *The* ability to love someone else flows directly from our love relationship with God.

During the early years of ministry, God used a special lady, Danita Estrella, to bring full restoration into the area of female relationships. Just at a time when I needed help in dealing with an ever-growing list of responsibilities, God spoke to me that Danita would be just the person to assist me and that she would do so with trust and integrity. He assured me that she could be entrusted with the most valuable aspects of my life—my family and my anointing. God spoke to Danita too, and she laid down her life and her own dreams to help me with my life and my dream. Like Jonathan and David, God knitted our hearts and souls together. Danita helped to reveal another important aspect of God's love for me. Presently she is a missionary in Haiti and has a wonderful children's orphanage.

The Greatest Love of All

What is the greatest love of all? It is the love God has for us. And what is the love of God? Paul wrote:

> Though I speak with the tongues of men and of angels, and have not charity, I am become as sounding brass, or a tinkling cymbal. And though I have the gift of prophecy, and understand all mysteries, and all knowledge; and though I have all faith, so that I could remove mountains, and have not charity, I am nothing. And though I bestow all my goods to feed the poor, and though I give my body to be burned, and have not charity, it profiteth me nothing.
>
> Charity suffereth long, and is kind; charity envieth not; charity vaunteth not itself, is not puffed up, doth not behave itself unseemly, seeketh not her own, is not easily provoked, thinketh no evil; rejoiceth not in iniquity, but rejoiceth in the truth; beareth all things, believeth all things, hopeth all things, endureth all things.
>
> Charity never faileth: but whether there be prophecies, they shall fail; whether there be tongues, they shall cease; whether there be knowledge, it shall vanish away.
>
> —1 CORINTHIANS 13:1–8

Love is patient. It is in no hurry. It suffers long, bears all things, believes all things, and endures all things.

Love is kind. It never acts rashly. It is not inconsistent or proud.

Love is generous. It is not envious or jealous.

Love is humble. It assumes no airs and does not parade itself. It does not act with ulterior motives or manipulate in order to receive something in return.

157

Love is polite. It is courteous and well mannered. It has equality with all classes.

Love is not rude. It is not suspicious or abusive.

Love is unselfish. It is not bitter or revengeful. It seeks only the good of others.

Love has a good disposition. It is never irritated or resentful.

Love is righteous. It hates sin. It is never glad when others go wrong. It is eager to believe the best in others.

Love is sincere. It is not boastful or conceited. It is honest. It is always hopeful and endures all things.

Can you imagine being loved this way? Well, you are! The love God has for you is unconditional, unwavering, and irrevocable. It surpasses powers of understanding or reason. It is everlasting, free, and enduring until the end. And how glorious! God has given this love to you and to me.

There is great joy in giving God's love to others, for He affirms that it is more blessed to give than to receive. When you comprehend and receive the love of God, then you can freely give the love of God. The ability to love someone else flows directly from our love relationship with God.

Life really only begins when we know that we are loved by someone just as we really are—flaws and gifts, weaknesses and strengths, good and bad. Only God's love provides the contentment and fulfillment for which we have searched. God loves us because of who He is, not because of who we are. He does not just offer love, He *is* love!

God will never become bored or tired of you. He will never abandon you or reject you. He will never leave you for a more exciting lover. His love is constant. It is in experiencing His love that we find ourselves. In His love, we discover our worth, our identity, and our significance. We in turn love Him, because He has first loved us.

Personal Reflections

Think About This

Read the quotes from this chapter below. After each one take a moment to reflect on how the statement links to a feeling or experience in your own life. Give your own personal reaction to each statement.

1. Once you experience God's love for yourself, you will understand that no thing, no being seen or unseen, no situation, no circumstance, no attack—absolutely *nothing*—can separate you from the love of God. Tell how God has demonstrated His love for you.

_____

_____

_____

_____

_____

_____

_____

2. The author states: "I love to give. It is one of my greatest joys in life." On pages 154–156 the author shares how God taught her to give her love by loving other women. Share an example from your own life that demonstrates how God has shown you how to give of yourself to another person.

_____

_____

_____

_____

_____

_____

_____

3. Life really only begins when we know that we are loved by someone just as we really are—flaws and gifts, weaknesses and strengths, good and bad. Only God's love provides the contentment and fulfillment for which we have searched. In your answer to this final "Personal Reflections" question, tell how God has provided you with contentment and fulfillment in places where you used to feel only pain and loss.

_____

_____

_____

_____

_____

_____

_____

Talk to God

> _Lord, remove every scale from my eyes, remove every blinder, remove every blockage that has kept me from accepting the truth about Your love for me. I confess and affirm that You love me in spite of my imperfections, in spite of my sins, in spite of everything I have ever done against myself, against others, or against You. I freely receive the gift of love_

You offer me, and I ask You to remove any fear that blocks me from receiving Your love or the love of others. Lord, show off in my life and demonstrate Your love to me. Bring healing, restoration, blessing, power, and godly relationships. Use these to reveal Your love to me. Reassure me that the game "he loves me, he loves me not…" is unnecessary in my life, for You have always loved me, You love me now, and You always will. Amen.

About the Author

Pastor Paula White is known for her dynamic Bible teaching and preaching. She communicates the exciting message of Christ with sincerity and intensity and is recognized for her ability to convey the concrete realities of God's Word for today.

Paula, along with her husband, Dr. Randy White, is co-pastor and co-founder of Without Walls International Church (formerly South Tampa Christian Center), a thriving, multi-racial expression of some 15,000 in the Tampa Bay area. This church has been recognized as one of the fastest growing churches in the nation today. Without Walls International Church has established nearly 270 ministries, many of which extend to inner-city families, the homeless, the needy, and the elderly. Pastor Paula has also been instrumental in establishing a medical center, an adoption agency, Christian academy, vocational and technical center and ministerial internship certification institute.

Paula hosts a nationally syndicated TV program, *Paula White Today*, which can be seen on Black Entertainment Television (BET), Trinity Broadcasting Network (TBN), The Church Channel, The Miracle Network, Court TV, Word Network, and Daystar Television Network. Her program is seen not only in America, but also in Canada and around the world. In addition, she co-hosts a daily TV program entitled *Without Walls* with her husband, Randy, in Tampa, Florida.

Paula has formal education in Ministerial Studies, Christian Education, and has an honorary doctorate degree. Paula created an accredited curriculum for Master Pastor Internship Program, a nine-month practicum in ministerial studies. She co-founded *Operation S.T.I.T.C.H.E.S.* (Saving The Inner Cities Through

Christ's Hope Eternal Salvation) in 1992. *Operation S.T.I.T.C.H.E.S.* was first introduced to the riot-stricken areas of Los Angeles where over 50,000 people gave their hearts to the Lord during a one-month period.

Through conferences, retreats, crusades, outreaches, and television, Paula White Ministries has led over one million souls to Christ. Paula travels around the globe teaching and preaching the Word of God. Her heart's cry is to transform lives, heal hearts, and win souls all for the glory of God.